Human Finitude
and Interreligious Dialogue

Mega Hidayati

Adelaide
2010

Text copyright © 2010 remains with the author.

All rights reserved. Except for any fair dealing permitted under the Copyright Act, no part of this book may be reproduced by any means without prior permission. Inquiries should be made to the publisher.

Cover design by Astrid Sengkey

An imprint of the ATF Ltd
PO Box 504
Hindmarsh, SA 5007
ABN 90 116 359 963
www.atfpress.com

Contents

Preface

It was in March of 2003, during the first class of the first course that I taught at the Center for Crosscultural and Religious Studies in Yogyakarta, that I first met Mega Hidayati. Hers was one of the many smiling, eager female faces in class, almost all of them framed in colorful jilbabs. It was only a few days later, when she came to my office to talk about her Master's thesis, that I realised how different this smiling face was. Her announcement just about knocked me off my chair: 'I would like to write a thesis on Hans-Georg Gadamer's understanding of human finitude and dialogue?'

Gadamer? A German philosopher, well-known in the West, relevant for his hermeneutical theory, deep but also complex and often stuffy. Why would a young Muslim Master's student—exceptionally bright but also deeply religious and thoroughly Indonesian—be interested in Gadamer? In that first conversation, in which she outlined why she felt that this Teutonic hermeneut had something to say to the multi-religious, multi-traditioned society of Indonesia, I came to an appreciation of Hidayati that has only deepened over the next few years of advising her for her thesis. (Those years were a bit extended since she interspersed them with marriage and the birth of a son.)

Another surprise came shortly after she arrived here at Union Theological Seminary in August 2009 to be the first doctoral student in an exchange program between the newly formed Indonesian Consortium for Religious Studies in Yogya and our school. Modestly, almost casually, she informed me that her thesis was going to be published and that she would be greatly honored if I could write a Preface for it. A Master's thesis published as a book, by a student whom I had the privilege of directing—I assured her that the honor was must greater for me than for her.

And an honor it is, not only because this book is an exceptional publishing achievement but also because it is a significant, creative contribution to the discussion about religious pluralism and interreligious engagement, both for Indonesia and around the world. In this, her 'Gadamerian-Indonesian conversation', Hidayati has identified and interpreted what Gadamer has to say to theologians, both Christians and Muslims, who are trying to work out a theological and dialogical understanding of the religious other. At the same time, and more broadly, she clarifies the help Gadamer might offer to her fellow Indonesian citizens who are committed to fashioning Indonesia into an ever-more flourishing multi-religious culture and nation.

But it is the philosophical and consequentially the theological foundations for religious pluralism and engagement that receive the bulk of Hidayati's attention in the pages that follow. In a sense, she mines the complex content of Gadamer's philosophy of human finitude and hermeneutics and finds the building materials for what might be called a 'Gadamerian Theology of Religions and Religious Dialogue'. As I read her, I believe that she offers two essential foundation stones for such a theology: Gadamer's case for both the *necessity* and the *difficulty* (even *danger)* of interreligious and cross-cultural engagement. Both necessity and difficulty are grounded in the focus of Hidayati's conversation with Gadamer: his understanding of what she calls 'human finitude'.

For Gadamer, and as is clear for Hidayati, our human finitude and condition is such that even though we are well equipped to know what is true, our equipment is such that we can never know the truth totally or with unquestioned accuracy. Our quest for truth is just that—*ours,* never just *mine.* Our human finitude is a tradition-born-and-bred identity. We are always approaching, perceiving, comprehending the real within the context of, and through the lens of, our own tradition. And this tradition, this situatedness and social-constructedness, enables us to see and under-stand. But it also, at the same time, limits what we see and understand.

Thus, the necessity of engaging other traditions. Our limited, tradi-tion-bound, vision can be expanded through the limited, tradition-bound visions of the other. What we do no see, they might see. And of course, vice-versa. As Gadamer put it, our limited horizons are not just expand-able, they are capable of merging or melting with other horizons (*Hori-*

zontverschmelzung). (Though I do not think he ever made a clear case as to *why* that is so.)

But the merging or melting is not always easy. And herein lies the difficulty that can all too easily become a danger. We always approach the other from our own traditioned standpoint; we have no other choice or possibility. And there is the dangerous rub: If we have to view the other only through our own perspective, how is it possible to see what is *not* contained in our own perspective—what is perhaps beyond it or in apparent opposition to it? Herein we face the difficulty, the unavoidable difficulty, of 'melting' or expanding our viewpoint so that it can understand what is *beyond* it, what is truly other than it. This difficulty becomes dangerous when, in not being able to—or, in refusing to—expand our horizon, we end up imposing it on the other. And if our traditioned perspective or culture is more powerful than the other—economically, militarily—then what was only an epistemological imposition becomes an imperial exploitation.

Because such dangers of imposition and exploitation are so real, because there is such an evident historical record of their horrible reality (both in the time of colonialism and post-colonialism!), there are many—especially among the postmodernists—who negate the necessity of dialogue because of its dangers.

Hidayati traces this back and forth, this give-and-take, between the necessity and the difficulty/danger of interreligious and intercultural engagement in her application of Gadamer's hermeneutics to the contemporary discussion about theologies of religions. Here, I feel honored and challenged by the conversation she carries out between Gadamer and the four models for Christian views of other religions, which I lay out in my *Introducing Theologies of Religions* (in its Indonesian translation: *Pengantar Teologi Agama-Agama,* Penerbit Kanisius, 2008). (I discovered in teaching these models at CRCS that they are also applicable to Muslim efforts to fashion an Islam theology of religions.)

And when I find myself questioning her cautious conclusion that Gadamer would be most comfortable with what I call the postmodern 'Acceptance Model' (that is because my preferences lie with the 'Mutualist Model'), I realise that Hidayati has successfully engaged me in the task that she is trying to promote—a more explicit, a more honest, and a more globally responsible conversation among all religions about how we can respect each other, learn from each other, avoiding exploiting each other, and cooperate in addressing the pressing needs of our planet and its children.

I hope and I expect this book to be an important contribution to the global effort to bring the *many religions* together for the well-being of our *one earth*. And I suspect, and hope, that this will be only the first of Mega Hidayati's contributions.

Paul F Knitter
Paul Tillich Professor of Theology, World Religions, and Culture
Union Theological Seminary, New York City

Acknowledgments

This monograph is based on my Master's thesis at Center for Religious and Cross-Cultural Studies (CRCS). Certainly, this writing would have been completely impossible without the support and the help of many people. I realise that my expression of thanks in words is not enough to describe how much I owe to those people.

First of all, I would like to thank to the chairman of Center for Religious and Cross Cultural Studies, Prof Dr Achmad Mursyidi who afforded me the opportunity to take part this program. I owe my thanks to Dr Irwan Abdullah, the Executive Director of CRCS at that time, for advice and encouragement. I also would like to express my thanks to lectures in CRCS who have introduced me to religious studies. I would also like to thank to Dr Zainal Abidin Bagir, the Executive Director of CRCS who recommended that this monograph be published and to ATF Press the publisher.

In addition, my thanks are due to my advisors, Professor Bernard Adeney-Risakotta PhD, and Professor Dr Paul F Knitter. They have given me many great suggestions and have shared their insights during my study. The idea of this study came from Knitter's class when he taught at CRCS during 2003. The idea just suddenly came to my mind one day when he described his typology of interreligious dialogue. I found that Hans-Georg Gadamer's thoughts on human finitude also provided contributions in viewing Kinitter's typology. My passion for interreligious dialogue began in this class and Professor Knitter was the first person who introduced me to the topic. Therefore, I am also very happy when he agreed to write the preface for this book.

I am indebted also to Professor Dr John Raines for his advice, information, dialogue and intellectual stimulus. I discussed my proposal and the problem of lack of primary and secondary sources with him. I said that I needed several books that were not available in Indonesia. He asked me to make a list of the books based on priority since he would bring the books back when he came to Indonesia. He brought ten books which were really significant to my study. I also would like to thank Professor Dr Gisela Webb for the discussion we had and her encouragement.

I would like to thank to my three brothers and sister for their support and encouragement. I would also like to express my thanks to my family in-law and to my friends who have shared in caring my child, Adzka Mohammad Crosamer (at that time he was less than one year old), and to many people who cannot be mentioned here.

I am most grateful to my father, Roesdi Zainun, and my mother, Syahnizar, for their endless patience, encouragement, and prayer. Finally, I would like to thank to my very uncomplaining husband, Khairurijal Semendaye, for sharing in joys. Above all, I express gratitude to Allah for everything.

Background to the Topic and Introduction

Outline

There are various aspects to this brief study. The first, is to explore Gadamer's concept of human finitude and his offering of a model of dialogue. The second, is to outline the concept of human finitude and interreligious dialogue by associating it with Paul Knitter's four models of interreligious dialogue. The third aspect to this study is to examine inter-religious dialogue with particular reference to the multicultural multi-religious state of Indonesia. This is a country with the largest Muslim population in the world, but a state which celebrates other religious festivals and feast days. But, at the same time is a country which has had its large share of multi-religious differences and acts of terrorism over the years and in recent times.

Introduction

The world is always changing with developments in science and technol-ogy, particularly in the areas of communication and transport. This often leads to the disappearance of 'boundaries' between states. In addition, cul-tural and religious encounters are common place, leading human beings to a realisation that they live in a pluralistic world; a pluralism of cultures, ethnicities and religions. As Knitter emphasises, people once considered as strangers now become neighbors.[1]

---

1. Paul F Knitter, *Introducing Theologies of Religions* (Maryknoll, NY: Orbis Books, 2002), 5.

This reality has led to the now almost universally used term of a 'global village', a term which was popularised by Marshall McLuhan.[2] Put simply, this term means that people find that while they have different cultures, ethnicities and religions they live together in one place. Or, as Swidler writes, the world has become 'everyman's living room'.[3] An awareness of this situation should lead all human beings to find values and norms which will bring lead them to a peaceful life. However, this is not simple task. Every culture and religion has its own claim on the truth about how human beings should live in the world. Religious belief has perhaps one of most important positions in relating to truths, values, and norms. As Kurtz suggests:

> The process of coming together, however, will not be an easy one. Religious traditions are central to that process because their role in defining norm, values and meaning; in providing the ethical underpinning for collective life; and in forging the cultural tools for cooperation and conflict.[4]

This plurality of world religions has made us aware of the existence of different ways of life. Every person is free to choose what he or she considers is the right path, the right way of life. The problem is that one usually employs his or her beliefs in viewing and judging other people beliefs. Knitter argues that each person has his/her own telescope, representing his/her own culture or religion, through which they to see and observe others. But what can be described as a so-called righteousness extends only as far as the area this telescope reaches. We need other telescopes to extend the reach of our own telescope. In other words we need the reach of other's telescopes, because 'the truth that we see through our own cultural religious telescope is not only limited but dangerous'.[5] This suggests that humans are also limited in their understanding of others' beliefs.

The question is how does one react towards others' convictions in such a way to avoid conflict and violence? On the one hand, humans are faced with a pluralistic world, but, on the other, there are urgent issues which

2. Lester R. Kurtz, *God in Global Village: the World's Religions in Sociological Perspective* (California: Pine Forge Press, 1995), 4.
3. Leonard Swidler, *After the Absolute: The Dialogical Future of Religious Reflection* (Minneapolis: Augsburg-Fortress Press, 1990), 12.
4. Kurtz, *God in Global Village*, 2.
5. Knitter, *Introducing Theologies of Religions*, 11.

remain to be solved together such as starvation, poverty, peace, human rights, discrimination and justice. Cooperation between religious societies is necessary to overcome problems arising amidst this plurality without having to unite into one religion. The religious area is not only a matter of fact but also a matter of principle, as Knitter, has argued.[6] Dialogue is an important medium to learning and to understanding others. Dialogue, he suggests, is the way to avoid violence and conflict, and to maintain peace. However, dialogue it is not unproblematic. For, as Knitter suggests 'the human race is constructing a multicultural global village full of conflict and violence as well as promise'.[7] All religions have a significant role in this problem. Hans Kung also has subscribed to this, believing in the importance of dialogue between world religions.[8]

In Indonesia, the encounter of various cultures, religions and ethnicities is inevitable within a country of so many different racial and religious groups; one which is spread out over such a vast area, an archipelago of so many different islands. This is a potential ground for conflict as is well documented over recent years: Maluku, Poso, Tasik Malaya, and North Sumatra.

Garang argues that ethnic, racial and religious sentiments increase and expand in Indonesian, and that religious sentiment is the most dominant of these.[9] There are many theories which try to explain these conflicts. Many theories focus on politics as the main reason, but I believe religious difference is also a major aspect and that interreligious dialogue is a central element in avoiding these conflicts.

Based on this brief description, I believe that human finitude has an important role in leading to different concepts of truth which can, on the one hand potentially lead to conflict and violence, but on the other can lead to dialogue which can then bring about peace. I find that Hans-Georg Gadamer's concept of human finitude contributes significantly, at a theoretical level, to the task involved in interreligious dialogue and is why I have used his work in this study.

---

6. *Ibid*, 7–8.

7. Kurtz, *God in Global Village*, 2.

8. He writes that 'no peace among the nations without peace among the religions; no peace among the religions without dialogue among the religions'. Hans Kung, *Global Responsibility: in Search of a New World Ethic* (New York: Crossroad, 1991), 138.

9. J Garang, in John Pieris, *Tragedi Maluku: Sebuah Krisis Peradaban* (Jakarta: Yayasan Obor, 2004), 17.

Hans-Georg Gadamer

Hans-Georg Gadamer was born in Marburg, Germany in 1900. He was a son of a professor of pharmacology and chemistry, Johannes Gadamer. Unlike his father, Hans-Georg Gadamer was more interested in literature, art, history, philology, language and philosophy.

Gadamer studied philosophy at the University of Breslau, Germany. While he studied under neo-Kantian's he was, however, more interested in Greek philosophy, and wrote his doctoral dissertation on Plato.

Several months after finishing his dissertation, Gadamer was isolated at home due to a polio infection. During his isolation, he read two manuscripts, Huserl's 'Logical Investigations' and Heidegger's 'Phenomenological Interpretation of Aristotle (Indication of the Situation in Hermeneutics)'. In the summer semester of 1923, soon after recovering from his illness, Gadamer decided to take up study at Freiburg where Heidegger was then teaching. He studied with Husserl and Richard Kroner. In that semester, Heidegger gave a lecture on the *Hermeneutics of Facticity*[10] in which emphasised that human existence, or *Dasein,* is limited by its culture. His thought was elaborated later in his book *Being and Time.*[11]

The encounter with Heidegger in 1923 was the beginning of Gadamer's interest in hermeneutics. Gadamer attended all of Heidegger's classes and became his assistant from 1923 till 1934.

In 1928, Gadamer finished his *Habitlitaionsschrift* titled *Plato's Dialectical Ethic*[12] which was supervised by Heidegger. This enabled him to teach and then became *Privatdozen* in classical philosophy and ethics at Marburg until he moved to Kiel in 1934. In that year, 1934, his book *Plato's dialektishe Ethik* was published.

Gadamer moved back to Marburg and received a lower-level non civil service professorship in 1937. He achieved full professorship at Leipzig in

---

10. During twenties, Heidegger gave lectures in Freiburg and Marburg and he was exciting about hermeneutics. *The Hermeneutics of Facticity* is one of lectures in which he discussed the idea of hermeneutics.
11. Heidegger's Magnum Opus *Being and Time* was published in 1927. As Grondin has suggested, the title of this book wants to alert us about radical temporality of all beings. Jean Grondin, *Hans-Georg Gadamer: a Biography* (New Haven and London: Yale University Press, 2003), 2.
12. This writing contains Gadamer's earliest interpretations of Plato by asking 'whether and how Platonic dialectic is ethics'. Francis J Ambrosio, 'Gadamer, Plato, and the Discipline of Dialogue', in *International Philosophical Quarterly* XXVII/1 105 March 1987: 21. Gadamer's interpretations of Plato continued throughout his career, many writings have been published with Plato as the theme.

1939. There he taught Greek philosophy, other subjects related to the philosophy of Hegel, Kant, Nietzshe, modern philosophy and the principle of humanity.

From 1945 to 1947, Gadamer was Rector at the University of Leipzig, and soon after became a professor at the University of Frankfurt and taught there until 1949, when he moved to Heidelberg. He lived in that city until he achieved the status of Emeritus Professor, in 1968. After several years, Gadamer, finally, succeeded in completing his magnum opus *Wahrheit und Methode* in 1958, which was then published in 1960. The book was translated into several language in the 1920s.[13]

Wahrheit und Methode led many people to view Gadamer as an independent thinker, while previously they had thought of him as another Heidegger.[14] Even then, however, some people still viewed the book as a great contribution to Heidegger's *Being and Time*. Jurgen Habermas, for example, regarded Gadamer's hermeneutics as 'an urbanisation of Heideggerian countryside'.[15]

Following his retirement, Gadamer was invited to speak at various universities around the world: the United States, South Africa, Yugoslavia, Naples, Italy, Poland, and several European nations. Gadamer died in Heidelberg in March 2002.

Gadamer and Heidegger

Gadamer's thought is close to Heidegger's hermeneutics of facticity. According to Gadamer, human knowledge and even human practices are influenced more by human tradition and prejudice, that is, human finitude. Gadamer can be considered as a postmodern philosopher in the sense that he questions the evidence of modernity, but Gadamer also criticises postmodernism which he believed unconsciously became Cartesian.[16]

Gadamer does not discuss the relationship between method and truth but criticises the monopoly of method in truth. In other words, method does not consider human finitude and does not view the possibilities of human awareness.[17] Comeron argues that Gadamer 'is not anti-method-

---

13. Grondin, Hans-Georg Gadamer: A Biography, 291.
14. *Ibid*, 2.
15. *Ibid*, 6.
16. Jean Grondin, *The Philosophy of Gadamer* (Montreal & Kingston, Ithaca: McGill-Queen's University Press, 2003), 2–3.
17. *Ibid*, 3.

ological but rather wishes to go deeper'.[18] Gadamer himself offers herme-neutical methodology in arguing against the methodology of natural science.

Relating Human Finitude to Interreligious Dialogue

In this study I use Gadamer's ideas on human finitude and examine them in relation to interreligious dialogue. Paul Knitter's ideas of four models of interreligious dialogue are analysed through Gadamer's concept of human finitude. These models are comprehensive model in discussing the phenomena of interreligious dialogue.

In *Introducing Theologies of Religions*[19] Knitter states that there are four models of interreligious dialogue. These are replacement, fulfillment, mutuality, and acceptance. The explanations for these four are as follows.

1. Replacement: This model states that there is only one right world religion so other religions need to be replaced totally or partially by the right one. This model believes that an absolute truth or final truth does exist. There are several reasons from politics, philosophy, culture and religion that support this model. For example, there is a belief that God acknowledges only one right religion, as often mentioned in holy books of various religions. When social conflict or confrontation occur, to overcome this human beings need one right rule that is admitted as a common consensus; human beings need one clear center to act together and interact with each other. That one clear center is God's given path. This model convinces us that human beings need more than just one truth but God's given truth as well. This model, moreover, opposes the view that the final truth is impossible to be achieved. It also stresses that because something is difficult to achieve does not mean that it does not exist.

This model, in addition, offers 'holy competition' in dialogue. This means that every participant shows why his or her religion becomes the best one, and can properly overcome all problems of humanity. Nevertheless, the dialogue in this model flows naturally, helpfully, and with love. Dialogue has always been persuading, inviting, attractive and respecting.

2. Fulfillment: In comparison to the first model, in this model there is a shift concerning the view of one religion towards other religions. This model believes that God's love is universal and particular; it is universal

---

18. WSK Cameron, 'On Communicative Actors Talking Past One Another: The Gadamer-Habermas Debate', in *Philosophy Today*. Spring, 1996: 11.

19. Knitter, *Introducing Theologies of Religions*, 19–237.

in terms of revelation and of God's existence that is also available in other religions. Because of that, values and truths may be found in other religions. God sent a prophet or messenger, prophet or a guru, to correct, and to improve the human-God relationship or to remind them to follow God's path. In this sense, there is no salvation in other religions because it has been fulfilled by one religion that has absolute superiority, savior and guarantee. In this second model other religions are viewed as a ray of truth or ways of salvation. As a ray of truth they never achieve the fullness of salvation. Other religions are viewed as preparation for salvation. The reason for this model is that people need one symbol of truth and one criterion of truth. Moreover, the dialogue offered is still considered as a holy competition, although openness is more evident compared to the commitment. The lesson acquired through dialogue is none other than to deepen the understanding and knowledge of the religious adherent.

3. Mutuality: This model focuses on the universality of God's love. Thus, the steps taken in this model are (1) to distance oneself from absolute claims of truth, (2) to pursue common issues found within religions, and (3) to distance oneself from relativism. In this model, religious uniqueness or non-negotiable issues can still be reinterpreted. Dialogue through this model is viewed as an ethical imperative. The fact that all religions call upon all human beings to love each other will be of no use due to the other fact that we will not be able to love someone unless we strive to listen, respect, understand, and learn from him/her. This clarifies that the relationship is considered more important to plurality in this model.

This kind of dialogue needs a level playing field, meaning that the participants involved in the dialogue must be considered as equals and also a common ground for dialogue must be available. Some examples regarding common issues for dialogue are: (1) common sense in relation with eco-human suffering, which is responded to by all religions, and (2) common mystical experiences.

Acceptance: According to this model, the differences existent in the religions are not meant to be and cannot be united: the many cannot be one. The fact that we are very different is something we need not avoid since there is no tool available to measure the perspective of others. Therefore, universal truth is impossible and dangerous: to say that a universal truth exists means abolishing other cultures. Universal truth is metanarrative from an understanding of narrative which is not detachable from cultural and religious influences. Each religion respectively differs in many issues such as (1) language and experience, (2) final goal, and (3) salvation. Thus there is no common ground within religions.

The dialogue offered then is a good neighbor policy, meaning that we talk to each other, help each other, and try to cooperate with each other, nevertheless still keeping in mind that we must stay in our own respective territory and not cross into the theological territories of other religions. We must accept the fact that each religion has its own claims of truth and this is what create its distinctive character and differentiates it from the others. In this dialogue, we are able to learn a lot from other religions and this will also bring us to a better understanding of our own religion.

Summary and Outline

There are various aspects to this brief study. The first is to explore Gadamer's concept of human finitude and his offering of a model of dialogue. The second is to the concept of human finitude and interreligious dialogue by associating it to Knitter's ideas of the four models of interreligious dialogue. The third aspect to this study is to examine interreligious dialogue with particular reference to the multicultural multi-religious state of Indonesia. This is a country with the largest Muslim population in the world, but a state which celebrates other religious festivals and feast days, but is country which has had its large share of multi-religious differences and acts of terrorism.

Gadamer's Concept of Human Finitude

This chapter is divided into two parts. The first part examines what Gadamer means by human finitude. The second part discusses the implication of Gadamer's ideas of human finitude on human understanding and the concept of truth.

Human Finitude in Tradition, Experience, and Language

For Gadamer, the limitations of being human are all too apparent in tradition, experience, and language.

Gadamer's thoughts on tradition begins with his objections to ideas of the intellectual figures at the time of the Enlightenment, especially the importance of reason and tradition. He argues that Romanticism failed in its efforts to argue against reason and tradition.

In Gadamer's view, we are indebted to Romanticism since the thinkers of this period held that tradition can held up as being true, but to say that tradition has been provided by history is unacceptable because tradition is an element of history itself.[1] Accordingly, Romanticism is incapable of providing a sufficient concept of tradition, one which is as a reaction against Enlightenment thought, because the principles they use are still in line with the paradigms of the Enlightenment. If tradition is regarded as a result of history, it means that tradition remains in function until today

---

1. Hans-Georg Gadamer, 'The Historicity of Understanding,' in Kurt Mueller Volmer. *The Hermeneutics Reader: Texts of the German Tradition from Enlightenment to the Present* (New York: Continuum, 1985), 265.

because the power of reason keeps it intact. In contrast Gadamer rejects both concepts of tradition:

> We stand always within tradition, and this is no objectify-
> ing process, that is, we do not conceive of what tradition
> says as something other, something alien. It is always part of
> us, a model and exemplar, a recognition of ourselves which
> our later historical judgment would hardly see as a kind of
> knowledge, but as simplest preservation of tradition.[2]

Thus, tradition is neither determined by reason nor a result of history, but it is a part of being human. The effort to objectify tradition, as the Enlightenment did, is a false one because the process of objectification means that tradition is understood as an object—something external. Contrary to Romanticism, tradition is not provided by history; instead, history is the result of the protected tradition. As a part of us, tradition is not only a precondition but we produce it; we are involved in the evolution of tradition.[3] For Gadamer, tradition is not the proof of validity because human finitude makes it impossible to demand proof.[4]

Besides this, Gadamer believes in the liberation of the fetter of time. He believes that distance, location, and thought guide human beings to attain the absolute.[5] It is a logical impossibility for human beings to exist in another particular space and time. Human beings came into the world where tradition has previously been constructed. This view is similar to Heidegger's hermeneutics of facticity.

Heidegger affirms that human beings are thrown into the world, and this becomes human existence from the time they are born until the time they die.[6] This means that nobody can choose what they want to be. Nobody can choose to be, for instance, an Indonesian woman or someone else in another place and time, or another culture, or in another place and time. Humanity, for Heidegger, is *Dasein* (being there) meaning that s/he is conditioned by history, by time, and by 'Being' itself.[7]

---

2. Hans-Georg Gadamer, *Truth and Method* (New York: Seabury Press, 1975), 250.

3. *Ibid*, 273.

4. Gadamer, 'The Historicity of Understanding', 286.

5. On this, see Patricia Altenbernd Johnson, 'Gadamer: Incarnation, Finitude, and the Experience of Divine Infinitude', in *Faith and Philosophy*, 10/4 October 1993: 539–551.

6. Martin Heidegger, *Being and Time* (New York: Harper & Row, 1962), 172–224.

7. *Ibid.*

Sustaining Heidegger's thought, Gadamer states that 'there is no place which does not see you',[8] and 'we are members of an unbroken chain through which the past addresses us'.[9] This means that wherever we are, there is always an 'identity' that is given to us. In addition, he emphasises that

> We always already have a certain character; no one is a blank sheet of paper . . . In every other respect, too, we know that nobody really is fully aware of the things that cause him or her to become who he or she is.[10]

Human beings are not able to escape from the prejudices of their age. The difference between Gadamer and Heidegger is that the former asserts that the human person belongs to a tradition while the latter claims that in the end all can be said by 'there it is'.[11]

The Enlightenment figures, Gadamer argues, destroyed the balance of the relationship between tradition and reason since they regarded reason as having the power to legitimise tradition.[12] Gadamer emphasised that the negative view which is provided by the intellectual figures of Enlightenment has to be 'rehabilitated'.[13] Tradition is not a mistake for humans, instead, it is part of the human condition, and the essence of being human.[14] Therefore, it has to be regarded positively. However, the act of dismissing tradition is vain because it means dismissing a part of the human being itself.

Based on this explanation Gadamer describes his concept of tradition in general. However, it seems he does not take into account different concepts of tradition such as cultural tradition. Gadamer only mentions cultural tradition in passing when he refutes Enlightenment thought on

8. Hans-Georg Gadamer, 'The Problem of Historical Consciousness', (Berkeley-Los Angeles-London: University of California Press 1979), 108.
9. *Ibid*, 145.
10. Richard E Palmer, *Gadamer in Conversation: Reflections and Commentary* (New Heaven & London: Yale University Press, 2001), 43.
11. Theodore Kisiel, 'The Happening of Tradition: The Hermeneutics of Gadamer and Heidegger', in *Man and World 2,* 1969: 20.
12. WSK Cameron, 'On Communicative Actors Talking Past One Another: The Gadamer-Habermas Debate', in *Philosophy Today,* Spring, 1996: 161.
13. Gadamer, *Truth and Method,* 250.
14. *Ibid.*

tradition, or that the important position of tradition does not mean that the cultural tradition has to be absolutised.[15]

Tradition comes from human experience. These experiences form ideas, values, and regulations in having relationships between humans, and also with the natural world. The experience of each individual becomes different because it is determined by numerous circumstances, such as education and family background. In Gadamer writings, these experiences show human finitude.

For Gadamer, the tendency of modern science to objectify everything also occurs in the realm of experience. Modern science considers experience to be valid only if each experience can be repeated fundamentally. For Gadamer, this concept cannot be accepted because it means erasing the historicity of the experience. Gadamer sustains Aristotle's concept of induction that experiences are regarded valid only if they do not oppose new experiences. This is not only applied in scientific matters or modern experiments, but also in daily life.[16]

Although valid experiences cannot oppose new experiences, this does not indicate that new experiences always correct old ones because Gadamer believes that 'every experience is confrontation'.[17] That is, new experiences challenge old ones. The result of the confrontation may be that the new one is truly experience which then replaces the old one or it just proves that the old one is truly experience. The problem is how can we know that it is a truly new experience? Gadamer asserts that there is a fusion of horizon which is a requirement of truly new experience. That is, there is a fusion of the subject's horizon and the object's horizon which leads to a larger horizon.[18] The object's horizon is related to its historcality.

Gadamer argues that experience itself will lead humans to be 'more open to new experience . . . Experience has the effect of freeing one to be open to experience'.[19] Gadamer adopts the *pathei manthos* maxim of Aeschylus to explain his thought. That is that humans learn wisdom through suffering which in turn leads them to being more knowledgeable. A valuable experience usually opposes our expectations. Hence, the

---

15. On this see Cameron, 'On Communicative Actors Talking Past One Another: The Gadamer-Habermas Debate'.
16. Gadamer, *Truth and Method*, 314.
17. Gadamer, 'The Problem of Historical Consciousness', 108.
18. Thomas K Carr, *Newman and Gadamer: Toward a Hermeneutics of Religious Knowledge* (Atlanta, Georgia: Scholars Press, 1996), 35.
19. Gadamer in *Conversation: Reflection and Commentary*, edited and translated by Richard E Palmer (New Haven and London: Yale University Press, 2001), 53.

transition from old to new tradition is not always smooth and often causes human suffering. This also becomes the background of an experienced man as Gadamer points out:

> The truth of experience always contains an orientation towards new experience. That is why a person who is called 'experienced' has become such not only through experiences, but it is also open to new experiences. The perfection of his experience, the perfect form of what we call 'experienced', does not consist in the fact that someone already knows better than anyone else. Rather, the experienced person proves to be, on the contrary, someone who is radically undogmatic; who, because of the many experiences he has had and the knowledge he has drawn from them is particularly well equipped to have new experiences and to learn from them. The dialectic of experience has its own fulfillment not in definitive knowledge, but in that openness to experience that is encouraged by experience itself.[20]

Thus, an experienced person is not someone who knows more as is commonly thought, but rather is someone who can open him/herself to all new experiences and s/he is capable of learning from those new experiences.

Even though humans have the ability to know which experiences are good, through learning from them, no experience can be repeated. What we learn from experience often involves radical transformation of our view points, thus, it is impossible to return to that experience. Concerning this view, Gadamer offers a process which is called *reversal consciousness*, meaning humans have the ability to regenerate the experiences which are considered to be true.[21]

The fact that humans are incapable of repeating again what has once been experienced and of controlling their experiences is evidence of human finitude. Therefore, according to Gadamer, the real experience is an experience in which there is an awareness of human limitations of power and knowledge which is based on reason. Gadamer wrote:

---

20. Gadamer, *Truth and Method*, 319.
21. Georgia Warnke, *Gadamer: Hermeneutics, Tradition, and Reason* (Cambridge: Polity Press, 1987), 3.

Thus experience is experience of human finitude. The truly experienced man is who is aware of this, who knows that he is master neither of time nor future. The experienced man knows the limitedness of all prediction and the uncertainty of all plans. In him is realised the truth-value of experience. If it is characteristic of every phase of the process of experience that the experienced person acquires a new openness to new experiences, this is certainly true of the idea of complete experience. It does not mean that experience comes to an end in it and a higher form of knowledge is reached (Hegel), but experience is fully and truly present for the first time. In it all dogmatism, which proceeds from the soaring desires of the human heart, reaches an absolute barrier. Experience teaches us to recognise reality. [22]

Humans who realise that they have limitations, are those who are really experienced human beings, and thus are able to predict or plan ahead. Nevertheless, they must also realise that their predictions and plans are not definite. One experience will lead to subsequent experiences but this does not mean that the subsequent experiences will complete the previous experiences and reach the highest experience. Gadamer argues that experiences are in sequence. Moreover, experience bring humans to recognise reality. Thus humans understand the good things which have to be maintained in their life. Human awareness of the limitations of tradition and experience will be visible in their medium, that is, in language in which both will live on.

An experience needs to be described in language. In other words, experiences are understood by translating that experience into their own linguistic horizon.[23] People try to find the right words to reveal their experiences because without doing this, the experiences become impossible to understand.[24] In addition, the desire of human beings to obtain the highest good of experience is displayed in language.[25]

---

22. Gadamer, *Truth and Method*, 320.

23. James S Hans , 'Hans-Georg Gadamer and Hermeneutics Phenomenology', in *Philosophy Today*, 22, 1978: 14 .

24. Kisiel, 'The Happening of Tradition: The Hermeneutics of Gadamer and Heidegger', 14.

25. Francis J Ambrosio, 'Gadamer, Pluto, and the Discipline of Dialogue', in *International Philosophical Quarterly* Vol. XXVII/1105 March 1987: 28.

Gadamer rejects the theory which states that language is the system of pure instrumental sign or that language is just a communication tool. It is true that language functions as a tool when communication occurs, but this is not the essential meaning of language. If we view words as mere signs, it will bring us farther away from the nature of language:

> A word is not a sign for which one reaches, nor it is a sign that one makes or gives to another, it is not an existent thing which one takes up and to which one accords the ideality of meaning in order to make something else visible through it. This is a mistake on both counts. Rather, the ideality of the meaning lies in the word itself.[26]

Gadamer asserts that language's true being only occurs in conversation, in the application of understanding between two people. He continues that language which is introduced as a just communication tool, is an artificial language for its reality and only takes place in the process of communication.[27]

Following Aquinas, Gadamer believes that words do not have the ability to completely represent human thought. Humans always lack words to show their ideas. This is the background of the variety of words. Moreover, the limit of language also shows the limitation of human intellect. 'No human words can perfectly express our mind . . . From this essential imperfection it follows that the human word is not one, like the divine word, but it must necessarily be many words.'[28]

This variety of words and languages reinforces people to have different concepts. Thus, language does not determine a person's thoughts, on the contrary, language has the ability to express what a person wants to say but the human mind is finite in finding words to express what is experienced.[29] The ability of language to express anything that a person wants to express is proved through the continual process of changes in language, and because language needs to change continuously, it shows that total under-

---

26. Gadamer, *Truth and Method*, 377.
27. *Ibid*, 404.
28. Gadamer, *Truth and Method*, 385.
29. 'Hans-Georg Gadamer and Hermeneutic Phenomenology', 10.

standing can never be reached. This idea reinforces Heidegger's phrase 'the sayable word receives its determination from the unsayable.'[30]

According to Gadamer, the main task of language, however, is not to express human thought but to express the object itself. This means that humans always try to find various words to describe an object. Therefore, signs in human language are various and flexible. They are flexible in that the same word in a language does not necessarily express the same thing; it designates different things and different expressions of the same object, and vice versa.[31] Hence Gadamer states that language is speculative in character, meaning that on the one hand words are a perfect mirror which reflect all of the objects in front of it, but on the other, language is also like the image-mirror which does not exist in appearance but it makes something understandable.[32] Gadamer explains that language does not become a mirror again if all is said and done, but rather is a 'continual definition and redefinition of our lives.'[33] Thus, in our life, we make a new definition for the old problem through language which consequently leads humans to act differently from previous people who faced the same problem. This process happens throughout human history.

The aforementioned brings another function of language: language represents or depicts reality. It is a mediator of awareness and reality which unveils the world. What is visible in the world is always reflected through language thus human understanding also relates to the limitation of language. We possess our world linguistically. 'Word and subject matter, language and reality, are inseparable and the limits of our understanding coincide with the limits of our common language.'[34] Because of this, language becomes the basis of all understanding, and 'understanding does not reach out and take hold of language, it is carried out within language.'[35] Thus, to have language is to have the world for language as a place where the meeting of the 'I' and world occurs. This is the reason someone who has different linguistic traditions will view the world in different ways.

---

30. Kisiel, 'The Happening of Tradition: The Hermeneutics of Gadamer and Heidegger', 23.
31. Hans-Georg Gadamer, *Philosophical Hermeneutics* (London: University of California Press, 1977), 60.
32. Ambrosio, 'Gadamer, Plato, and the Discipline of Dialogue', 27.
33. Gadamer, 'The Historicity of Understanding', 274–292.
34. David Linge, Hans-Georg Gadamer, *Philosophical Hermeneutics* (London: University of California Press, 1977), xxviii.
35. Palmer, *Gadamer in Conversation: Reflections and Commentary*, 37.

This thought is in line with Clifford Geertz who said that language is not only a valuable tool for us, even we could not be without language.[36]

In Gadamer's view, words are conversation, dialogue, question, and answer which produce the world. This is due to the fact that language is acquired through meaning, interpretation, and understanding of the world which is not free from prejudice. In other words, language is assimilation and interpretation of an event at the same time. Thus, humans cannot be separated from language and see it or see the world from an objective point of view; language is not a tool for human beings to manipulate the present world which is so full of meaning.[37]

The important position of language leads Gadamer to conclude: 'being that can be understood is language'.[38] This phrase, as Grondin argues, leads people to misunderstanding,[39] or, as Murchadha suggests, it has the tendency to claim the opposite.[40] However, Madison asserts that 'to say that being that can be understood is language is not to say that being is nothing but language'.[41] Grondin's explanation really helps us to understand the phrase:

> With language everything can be understood or that everything intelligible has to be expressible in words. This dictum is meant as a limitation: we understood only insofar as we find words for what is to be understood. But when is it that we can do that? Understanding means searching for words for everything that is to be understood and said.[42]

Gadamer explains this phrase as follows: 'to want to understand everything which will allow itself to be understood'.[43] As a result, understanding

36. Felix O Murchadha, 'Truth as a Problem for Hermeneutics: Towards a Hermeneutical Theory of Truth', in *Philosophy Today,* Summer 1992: 126.
37. Jeffrey F Bullock 'Preaching in a postmodern Wor[l]d: Gadamer's Philosophical Hermeneutics as Homiletical Conversation', *Christian Theological Seminary Research Group* http://home.apu.edu/~CTRF/paper/1997_paper/bullock.html.
38. Gadamer, *Truth and Method,* 432.
39. Jean Grondin, *Hans-Georg Gadamer: A Biography* (New Haven and London: Yale University Press, 2003), 289.
40. Murchadha, 'Truth as a Problem for Hermeneutics', 124.
41. Gary Brent Madison, 'Hermeneutics and (the) Tradition', in *Hermeneutic and the Tradition,* edited by Daniel O Dahlstrom (Washington: The American Catholic Philosophical Association, 1988), 170.
42. Grondin, *Hans Georg Gadamer: A Biography,* 289.
43. Gadamer, 'The Historicity of Understanding', 284.

cannot be seen as a process of human encounters with an object, but understanding is the way that humans exist. Thus, language has an ontological relevance. Humans live in confinement of a certain language and cultural root. Language creates a feeling of 'belongingness' for humans in this world and urges them to participate in it. This does not mean language restrains human capabilities; on the contrary, it in fact opens a room for the existence of humans in the world. Through language, humans experience their existence in the world in every field of life. Moreover, humans have the ability to subjugate the world, an ability that transcends geographical limits. Nevertheless, as mentioned before, our language is limited by our intellectuality and history as well as its continual development:

> Language is the record of finitude, not because the structure of human language is multifarious, but because every language is constantly being formed and developed, the more it expresses its experience of the world.[44]

Gadamer's thought on language becomes problematic since he regards words as both a sign, on the one hand, and, on the other, words are not a sign. In addition, words are also considered as a presence, but unfortunately Gadamer does not provide an adequate explanation concerning 'the word as presence is an actuality'.[45]

Consequences of Human Finitude on Human Understanding and the Concept of Truth

The fact of human finitude shown above does, however, bring several consequences in human thinking and life. This section addresses the consequences and the way to respond to them as shown by Gadamer. The first part of this section maps out the effect of human finitude on understanding. The second part discovers how human finitude influences views of truth. And the last part discusses how prejudice, caused by the human finitude, should be acted out in response.

Tradition as a Gate of Human Understanding

As mentioned in the preceding passages, Gadamer regards tradition as the fact of human finitude meaning that human beings cannot be separated

---

44. Gadamer, *Truth and Method*, 415.
45. Hans, 'Hans-Georg Gadamer and Hermeneutic Phenomenology', 18.

from tradition and always become a part of it. This fact relates adequately to other human finitudes: experience and language. According to Gadamer, tradition is an experience of viewing an object itself and the nature of tradition is in language. This shows that it is impossible for humans to go beyond the borders of tradition. In other words, humans cannot be free from their age's prejudice. Humans live and develop in a culture, which cannot be free from prejudice wherever they are.

Based on this Gadamer believes that the process of one's understanding is always in the scope of tradition and cannot be avoided to be anything but this since it is the consequence of humans as beings-in-the-world. Thus, for Gadamer, understanding is human's basic mode of being in the world, not human's activity.

For Gadamer, human sciences provide the foundations for the continuous development of tradition for they are affected by tradition. Gadamer maintains that natural science is the product of a tradition of interpretation. The norms and the standards of science are simple prejudices of tradition. Natural science, which is regarded to have objectivity, still involves tradition. This is because the standards, which are given by natural science, have been constituted in a certain tradition. Thus, the standard cannot be absolute as a common demand. Our objectivity of knowledge is limited by dependence on tradition. This dependence cannot be overcome by a method.

The human situatedness in tradition, according to Gadamer, should not be regarded in the same negative fashion of the Enlightenment. Tradition is not given to us, but is a result, a product, of ourselves. The fault of the Enlightenment philosophers is that they rejected tradition because it is regarded as the authority that determines truth. Another mistake is that for the sake of objectivity they set aside authority, as they mistakenly did toward prejudice. According to Gadamer, tradition is not an authority; it is a situation that cannot be rejected by humans because tradition is a part of who they are. Even, human experience will begin from tradition. Gadamer believes that the totality of human experience rooted in tradition will lead to truth. In contrast, this situatedness opens a gate for humans to understand their lives and, through understanding, the truth can be attained. In other words, humans understand because they have and a part of a tradition. Hence, tradition as a gate for human understanding, only happens within a shared tradition and people have to understand what is shared. For Gadamer, there would be no cultures if there was no shared tradition.

Gadamer believes that people cannot see understanding as a *tabula rasa* for presuppositions are bequeathed from tradition and also because tradition gives meaning to humans. Therefore, Gadamer emphasises that

> Understanding is not to be thought of so much as an action
> of one's subjectivity, but as the placing of oneself within a
> process of tradition, in which past and present are constantly
> fused. This is what must be expressed in hermeneutical the-
> ory, which is far too dominated by the idea of the process, a
> method.[46]

We have to keep in mind that when Gadamer says method, it means method in the Enlightenment's concept of the term. As mentioned in the previous chapter, method in the Enlightenment meant the method of the natural sciences. The Enlightenment thinkers believed that the method of natural sciences was the only proper method for all of the sciences. They stressed that the accuracy of the natural scientific method had been proven: it doe not involve human subjectivity which misleads, and it brings development in human life. They also emphasised that there is no chain reaction between the past and the present. Thus, for these thinkers, there was no division between the method of the natural sciences and the method of the social sciences. There were, of course, many objections to this thinking, especially concerning the different objects among the natural and social sciences. The object of the former is related to nature which can be predicted and controlled technically, whereas the object of the latter is related to human beings who act differently towards each other and this cannot be predicted or controlled technically. Human beings cannot be treated and understood in the same way as nature.[47] Besides the differences between the two, Gadamer also emphasised that natural science, which is claimed to free from the past, is actually truly associated with the past or tradition; it is the product of a tradition of interpretation.

Tradition enables human beings to have the ability to overcome problems that arise throughout human life, in view of the fact that tradition is a foundation for humans to understand their reality, although they do not realise it. This means that the 'real truth', Gadamer believes, exists in

---

46. Gadamer, *Truth and Method*, 258.
47. F Budi Hardiman, *Melampaui Positivisme dan Modernitas* (Yogyakarta: Kanisius, 2003), 56–58.

tradition. For Gadamer, 'the truth of tradition is like the present that lies immediately open to the senses'.[48]

According to Healy, this is the centre of Gadamer's thought, that the meeting and the fusion of traditions enlarge human's horizon of understanding.[49] However, for Gadamer, the horizon of the present brings that of the past which he states as a 'historically operative consciousness'.[50] This idea will be discussed in greater detail in the next section.

Gadamer's thoughts on tradition and on prejudice should not be interpreted to mean that Gadamer under-estimates the function of reason in human life. According to Gadamer, reason has a strong function in considering true tradition. Human experiences also seek reason's consideration when the experiences are faced with new experiences that are opposite to those previous experiences. Nevertheless, reason that has a role in human rationality does not stand freely; it is always connected to previous reasoning sequences as Cameron has written. 'For Gadamer does not claim that we never have good reason, but that our reasons are dependent on other reasons (and so on), and that the chain of reasons can never be fully secured in a universal insight'.[51] In addition, Gadamer states that 'Reason exists for us only in concrete, historical terms, ie it is not its own master, but remains constantly dependent on the given circumstances in which it operates'.[52]

Habermas criticises Gadamer's disregard that tradition itself needs to be judged.[53] Based on the explanation above, it seems that Habermas' criticism cannot stand up because for Gadamer we need reason to know true tradition, that is, tradition which is regarded useful for human life. This implies that tradition is also judged, but Gadamer also reminds us that reason which functions as a tool to judge tradition is influenced by previous reasoning sequences.

---

48. Gadamer, *Truth and Method*, 420.
49. Paul Healy, 'Situated Rationality and Hermeneutics Understanding: A Gadamerian Approach to Rationality', in *International Philosophical Quarterly*, XXXVI/2/142, June 1996: 160.
50. John P Hogan, 'Gadamer and the Hermeneutical Experience', in *Philosophy Today*, 20: 1976: 5.
51. Cameron, 'On Communicative Actors Talking Past One Another: The Gadamer-Habermas Debate', 165.
52. Gadamer, *Truth and Method*, 245.
53. Cameron, 'On Communicative Actors Talking Past One Another: The Gadamer-Habermas Debate', 165.

In my view, it is clear that what Gadamer tries to create is the balance between tradition and reason. However, since his thought on tradition is induced by his strenuous objection to the Enlightenment's concept of tradition, he seems to place tradition in an elevated higher position. As Guirlanda says, Gadamer appears to be the champion of tradition and Habermas continues to be the heir of the Enlightenment.[54] Nevertheless, I agree with Hans that Gadamer's thought becomes clear when he emphasises that human's knowledge is limited because of their limitations, but humans have the ability to know the world because it is possible to obtain a greater understanding of it.[55]

Understanding truth as possible

As previously mentioned, the position of the past for Gadamer is significant. Humans cannot be free from historical chains and for Gadamer 'people who believe they have freed themselves from their interwoveness into their *effective history* are simply mistaken'.[56] Gadamer calls *effective history* to describe how history functions in human life and shows that we belong to history. Concerning Gadamer's concept of *effective history,* Schuhman has written that

> 'Effective history' means that in all our understanding we are
> always already within the horizon of particular questions,
> prejudices, interest, and viewpoints which are codetermined
> by what we want to understand in its effective-historical in-
> fluence, ie, in its influence as tradition.[57]

Humans cannot consider themselves a-historical beings since they are part of history and human understanding starts from history. For Gadamer, this also shows human finitude as Madison has suggested:

> To take human finitude seriously means drawing out all phil-
> osophical consequences latent in the fact that man 'belongs'
> to history, that a human being is essentially a historical mode
> of being, which is to say, that man not only 'has' a history but

---

54. Paul FSC Giurlanda, 'Habermas' Critique of Gadamer: Does it Stand Up?', in *International Philosophical Quarterly*, XXVII/1/105 March 1987: 39.

55. See Hans, 'Hans-Georg Gadamer and Hermeneutic Phenomenology', 19.

56. Gadamer, *Gadamer in Conversation: Reflection and Commentary,* 45.

57. Gadamer, 'The Problem of Historical Consciousness', 41.

is a history, is a product and function of his history, a history which itself is being constantly and creatively rewritten in our attempts to appropriate our distanciated past.[58]

This thought also appears in Heidegger's writings. He believes that authentic *Dasein* exists historically where human beings live by involving the repetition which is showed by the past.

Certainly, not all people view the function of history clearly. Historians, usually, have the ability to look at how history functions and influences human life since they have a historical sense, meaning clear thought on historical horizon related to the past and present life of human beings. To realise *effective history* means we are always thrown in a circle of ongoing situation which is better for humans. However, whether humans are aware of it or not, the power of *effective history* works in human life. According to Gadamer, this ongoing situation will never be complete due to the essence of a human as an historical being.

The *effective history*, for Gadamer, is important in human understanding because essentially understanding is 'effective-historical relation'. This is described in the relationship of the past and the present horizons. Gadamer asserts that horizon moves as someone moves, thus horizon in the past which existed in the past always moves.

In fact the horizon of the present is being continually formed, in that we have continually to test all our prejudices. An important part of this testing is the encounter with the past and the understanding of the tradition from which we come. Hence the horizon of the present cannot be formed without the past . . . In tradition this process of fusion is continually going on, for there old and new continually grow together to make something of living value, without either being explicitly distinguished from the other.[59]

This fusion of horizon not only relates to the past and the present, but also becomes a requirement in dialogue which will be discussed in the next chapter of this study.

The concept of *effective history* should make humans realise that there is no 'seeing in the first place', or 'no seeing is as a pure meaning since it has been prejudiced with various things'.[60] What we see always has 'some

---

58. Madison, 'Hermeneutics and (the) Tradition', 171.
59. Gadamer, *Truth and Method*, 273.
60. Carr, *Newman and Gadamer: Toward a Hermeneutics of Religious Knowledge,* 32.

kind of definition' that is given by previous people. All things that come to us bring out a variety of interpretation, meaning, and others.

For Gadamer, reality proves that objectivism is an illusion. There is nothing that frees us from subjectivity. Gadamer provides a new definition of objectivism: 'What we are can term here as objectivity cannot be anything other than the confirmation of an anticipation which results even in the very course of its elaboration'.[61]

This has a consequence for the concept of truth. Following Heidegger's idea, Gadamer believes that truths are 'Being-uncovering'. For Gadamer, humans cannot come to truth by only focusing on the essence because truth is more of a historical process where complementation or correction is possible through ongoing processes. As a result, understanding is always changing and developing. This is comparable to William James' thought that truths are historical constructs, what is regarded as truth always depends on human previous project and practice. Gadamer's thoughts develops Heidegger's thought that history discloses the truth. However, for Gadamer, humans are in time and this leads to a number of consequences. As Murchadha has outlined Gadamers' thought:

> Being is in time. Beyond time, we cannot speak of anything being. Thus, to be is to become, for nothing in time is unchanging. Thus, there are no essential truths, only historical truths, truths of what was and what may be. The primary mode of reality is possibility, the structure of understanding is that of the projection of possibilities. This is the structure of Being in the world . . . Truth is meaningful reality. The meaning of reality is a meaning for us, for our existence. But openness to this meaning is not just passive, it is rather, creative.[62]

Thus, all opinion is relative because understanding, according to Gadamer, is incomplete and contains the seed of error. This seems to leave human beings in some doubt, as if it were useless to look for truth since all achievements seem to be relative. Nevertheless, Gadamer emphasises that hermeneutics guarantees truth because it discovers how truths are constructed and are built up. I agree with Gadamer that universal truth

---

61. Gadamer, 'The Problem of Historical Consciousness', 149–150.
62. Murchadha, 'Truth as a Problem for Hermeneutics: Towards a Hermeneutical Theory of Truth', 127.

exists in terms of the application of what is to be understood and truth becomes relative when humans try to understand it in a particular situation. Thus we will never stop to search for truth and that what we found is not universal truth but rather only possible truth. The facticity of humanity in history does not lead humanity to being passive, but on the contrary, it leads them to be creative. Unfortunately, however, as Murchadha states, Gadamer's characteristic of truth is uncertain.[63]

This concept of truth raises the problem of relativism and that hermeneutics resist cultural relativism and philosophical nihilism as strenuously as it also opposes metaphysical absolutism. According to Fairfield, to go 'beyond relativism and objectivism' we need a tool for rational adjudication, recognition to the history of our criteria, and the fallibility of our judgments.[64] In this sense, it seems that Gadamer's ideas take us beyond relativity and objectivism and as Hans says, Gadamer's philosophy does not lead to relativism, but rather to continuity.[65] Although for Cameron, Gadamer's thought cannot bring us beyond relativism, in my mind, when Gadamer believes that there is universal truth, he is excluded from relativism.[66]

Prejudices and the Need for Dialogue

In the encounter between humans, who always exist in their finitude, prejudice arises. Philosophers, scientists, and religious people have discussed prejudice in many ways. This is because prejudice relates to other important and fundamental things, such as truth, decision-making, and method. However, many questions are brought to the fore. For example, does prejudice lead humans to failure in viewing truth and in making decision? Does prejudice have to be avoided in order to attain truth?

Gadamer's thought on prejudice is described through his strenuous refusal to ideas of the Enlightenment. The intellectual figures of the Enlightenment period regarded prejudice as an authority and over-hastiness which leads humans to false decisions since it dissolves objectivity. Based on their belief in reason, prejudice has to be avoided in order to attain

---

63. *Ibid*, 122.
64. Paul Fairfield, 'Truth Without Methodologism: Gadamer and James', in *American Catholic Philosophical Quarterley*, LXVII/3, 1993: 286.
65. Hans, 'Hans-Georg Gadamer and Hermeneutic Phenomenology', 3.
66. Cameron, 'On Communicative Actors Talking Past One Another: The Gadamer-Habermas Debate', 165.

undistorted truth. Moreover, they regarded prejudice as 'unfounded judgment'. This idea, Gadamer believed, was caused by the Enlightenment's spirit of rationalism. Gadamer rejected the Enlightenment view by providing the definition of prejudice: 'Actually, prejudice means a judgment that is given before all elements that determine a situation has been finally examined'. [67] This definition shows that prejudice should not be avoided, in contrast; it has to be recognised. Even, prejudice has an important position that makes understanding possible. The following paragraphs will support this standpoint.

Everyone, however, knows that when s/he goes through a process of understanding, prejudices will arise. It is surely inevitable, for prejudice is a bias of human openness to the world. Nevertheless, it does not mean that prejudices have to be followed by abandoning things which are found when the process of understanding goes on.

Prejudices are biases of our openness to the world. They are simply conditions whereby we experience something—whereby what we encounter says something to us. This formulation certainly does not mean that we are enclosed within walls of prejudice and only let through the narrow portals those things that can produce a passing comment along the lines that 'nothing new will be said here'.[68]

Gadamer believes that prejudice does not limit human efforts in seeking the truth because prejudice is a natural effect of openness to the world. Even, prejudice is a place where humans make a beginning. Humans will encounter different cultures, languages, and traditions. The human experiences of these encounters will bring prejudices. Moreover, language comes to humans by bringing meanings, interpretations, and understanding of human beings, which are not free from prejudices.[69] Thus, the history of human life is not free from prejudices, even things speak to humans through prejudice.[70]

The failure of the figures of the Enlightenment period in viewing prejudice is that people who involve prejudices in their efforts to obtain true knowledge are actually proposing their own subjective opinions, resulting in mere human subjectivity. They want to understand tradition without prejudice. According to Gadamer, the freedom to have prejudices should

---

67. Gadamer, *Truth and Method*, 240.
68. Gadamer, *Philosophical Hermeneutics*, 9.
69. Bullock, 'Preaching in a Postmodern Wor[l]d: Gadamer's Philosophical Hermeneutics as Homiletical Conversation'.
70. Hogan, 'Gadamer and the Hermeneutical Experience', 6.

not be understood as saying that all prejudices are true, since human knowledge needs critical understanding. Acknowledging the existence of prejudice does not mean that humans do not need other things in searching for knowledge since not all prejudices are true: there are legitimate and illegitimate prejudices. This means that although prejudices are biases of humanities openness to the world, they do not indicate that humans are determined entirely by the prejudices, as Gadamer says: 'Our openness does not mean that we present ourselves as a blank slate ready to be inscribed'.[71] Prejudice comes to humans through tradition which creates their self understanding. Thus, 'Tradition influences our thinking and interpretations whether or not we will them to'.[72] Humans have to separate prejudices which can be regarded as the principle of life (legitimate prejudice) and ones which cannot (illegitimate prejudice). Therefore, for Gadamer, although prejudices are often in error, they can be correct, and thus are not necessarily done away with.[73] What we have to do is to seek out which are true and those that are not, which are wrong, that are found in the root of all human experience.

Gadamer believes that prejudice is not a false pre-judgment, but it is a part of a reality, which can be judged positively or negatively. Enlightenment philosophy assigned negative value to prejudice, that is, prejudice is regarded as the authority which has to be extinguished; prejudice causes humans not to have the ability to achieve objective truth; and prejudice leads to an over-hastiness in viewing something which causes decision making errors. In contrast, Gadamer states that if an authority is existent in pre-judgment, there is a possibility that an authority also becomes a source of truth. This is another fault of the Enlightenment. But the fact that prejudice, a pre-judgment, has this kind of precedence actually says nothing about whether it is right or wrong, or about whether it accords with the facts or not. A prejudice may be quite correct, but the Enlightenment thinkers considered all prejudice (that is, all pre-judgment, predetermined by tradition) as false because it they were willing to call as true only those judgments that had received the imprimatur of method.[74]

---

71. Gadamer, 'On the Circle of Understanding', in *Hermeneutics Versus Science? Three German Views*, edited and translated by John M Connoly and Thomas Keutner (Notre Dame, Indiana: University of Notre Dame Press. 1988), 167.

72. Carr, *Newman and Gadamer: Toward a Hermeneutics of Religious Knowledge*, 54.

73. Hans, 'Hans-Georg Gadamer and Hermeneutic Phenomenology', 11.

74. Joel C Weinsheimer, *Gadamer's Hermeneutic: A Reading Truth and Method* (London: University of California Press, 1985), 69.

Prejudice is only pre-judgment which needs other things to be stated as wrong or right. The problem of the Enlightenment philosophers is that they thought that all prejudices compromise the status of truth.

Thus, according to Gadamer, the Enlightenment philosophy only form a new authority, that is, of reason. That is, that reason has the authority to claim something is true. Moreover, the Enlightenment thinkers refuse prejudice by giving another prejudice, *prejudice against prejudice*,[75] that is the prejudice that prejudice will lead people astray in attaining the truth. To Gadamer, what the Enlightenment did was to besmirch prejudice and disfigure authority.[76]

What needs to be conducted by humans towards the reality of their prejudices is to understand it through dialogue so that humans can separate between legitimate and illegitimate prejudices. Moreover, people have to realise that human reason demonstrates its limitation and leads us to acknowledge that others can have a better understanding than we do.[77] Therefore, we have to suspend our prejudice until we have a good understanding through dialogue.[78] Yet, humans, before entering into a dialogue about their prejudices, need to realise that their consciousness does not start in emptiness, but it is always fulfilled by pre-judgment or prejudice. This is repeated constantly in every measure of understanding. What Gadamer wants, according to Carr, is 'to make the strong claim that all our knowing activity is tainted by prejudice, whether for good or for ill'.[79]

In summary, we have discovered that the appearance of human finitude in tradition, experience and language influence human understanding and leads humans to have different concepts of truth and as this raises prejudice and the need for dialogue. Therefore, in Gadamer's view, 'language, understanding, interpretation, experience, tradition, and what Gadamer calls *effective history* are all indissolubly bound together'.[80] This is the background of truth as 'here and now'. This should urge human beings to be creative in discovering what they truly need in this life. Undoubtedly, because it places humans in a much more relative state of being, it is not without problems, especially when it concerns religious issues, as there are many absolute truth claims in this particular area.

---

75. Gadamer, *Truth and Method*, 273.

76. *Ibid*, 247–248.

77. *Ibid*, 248.

78. *Ibid*, 266.

79. Carr, *Newman and Gadamer: Toward a Hermeneutics of Religious Knowledge*, 52.

80. Hans, 'Hans-Georg Gadamer and Hermeneutic Phenomenology', 7.

However, as Murchadha suggests, 'truths in context are less problematic than truths which attempt to transcend a specific context'.[81] Nevertheless, regardless of its problems, Gadamer's ideas provide massive contributions to interreligious dialogue. In the light of his hermeneutical discussion his ideas assist people to aware of their goals and demonstrates a method, a way of achieving them.[82] Following Hogan,[83] I believe that Gadamer's hermeneutics is 'ground breaking' which needs to be developed.

---

81. Murchadha, 'Truth as a Problem for Hermeneutics: Towards a Hermeneutical Theory of Truth', 123.

82. Guirlanda, 'Habermas' Critique of Gadamer: Does it Stand Up?', 40–41.

83. Hogan, 'Gadamer and the Hermeneutical Experience', 10.

Gadamer's Discipline of Dialogue

In the previous chapter I examined Gadamer's thoughts on human finitude and how human finitude has influenced human understanding and thought on truth. In this chapter I examine Gadamer's proposition of a proper discipline of dialogue which deals with the facts.

For Gadamer, the discipline of dialogue has a prominent position in reaching the truth. He stresses that the discipline of dialogue is an effective and universal criterion of truth. Gadamer refutes the Enlightenment figure's thought on objectivism as a criterion of truth. As described in the previous chapter, the debate of method occurs because there is a claim that natural scientific methods have to be applied in social science for the sake of objectivism. This idea began in the Enlightenment period and was continued by other thinkers into the twentieth century. The radical form can be found in Positivism Comte that argues the method of natural science is the only norm of science. In this objectivism is so extreme that there is no subjective role for science. The efforts to replace the role of the subject in sciences, particularly social science, brought forth three approaches namely phenomenology, hermeneutics and critical theory. Phenomenology stresses phenomena in human life which influences human awareness. This idea is influenced by Lambert, Hegel, Husserl, Heidegger, Hamilton, Hartmann, Max Scheler, Sartre and Merleau-Ponty. Hermeneutics concerns interpretative systems. Heidegger provides large contributions in forming this approach. Among other hermeneutic thinkers are Dilthey, Schleirmacher and Gadamer. Critical theory emphasises the role of awareness in changing objective structures. The analysis focuses on super-structural phenomena. This approach is supported by Frankfurt figures and Habermas.

This chapter is addressed to neither find the answer to the problem outlined above nor to discuss whether dialogue is an effective and universal criterion of truth, but to examine what kind of dialogue is offered by Gadamer concerning human finitude.

A helpful insight to understand Gadamer's discipline of dialogue is by associating it with Gadamer's support for Platonic dialectics which view dialogue as a way of living. In this view, dialogue makes us linger wherever we are and for us to be friendly to each other because we all are gathered as a community of free people. This situation shows what Socrates practiced as the existential discipline of dialogue: individuals share with each other through a solidarity in answering questions about the good, and justice in human life. In the following pages, I examine how Gadamer develops these two thoughts.

For Gadamer, there are two kinds of dialogue which occur in human life: dialogue with texts and dialogue between humans. The former is also known as translation and the latter is known as conversation. In this study we examine dialogue between human beings, or conversation, and in the following discussion, dialogue and conversation are utilised with the same intention.

Defining Dialogue

In his book *Truth and Method*, Gadamer provides a definition of conversation as 'a process of two people understanding each other'.[1] The definition seems to be simple but the process whereby people come to understand each other is achieved is not quite so simple.

Gadamer's focus on dialectics is the same as Horderlin's phrase that 'the dialogue which we are', that is, we are involved in a dialogue whereas the dialogue never drives us to be involved.[2] Gadamer asserts that dialogue is not a thing which we create but that we fall into it, and a conversation is where there is neither a leader nor the one who is led. The leader here means people who control conversation, where a fabricated conversation is possible and the result of the conversation has been known beforehand.

---

1. Hans-Georg Gadamer, *Truth and Method*, translated by Garret Barden and John Cumming (New York: Seabury Press, 1975), 347.
2. Jervolino, 'Gadamer and Ricoeur on the Hermeneutics of Praxis', in *The Hermeneutics of Action*, edited by Richard Kearney (London: SAGE, 1996), 66.

Since no one participant controls a conversation, what comes out from conversation cannot be known exactly. Perhaps, we can conjecture what will happen in a conversation but we cannot certainly be always sure. Besides that, we cannot say that a conversation is good or bad because there are various points of view involved in each conversation, and moreover the language which is used in conversation brings its own truth.

For Gadamer, however, conversation has an important position in human life because conversation is 'the essence of all authentic human understanding' and 'a hermeneutical act of self-improvement'.[3] Conversation makes a person understand something and that understanding hopefully drives them to be a better person as a result of applying improvements to who they are as people. In other words, humans, after engaging in conversation, will obtain something that makes them knowledgeable in something which in turn enhances who they are. For this reason Gadamer believes that a conversation does not relate to other peoples opinion/s but to one's own opinion/s.

A conversation is something one gets caught up in, something in which one gets involved. In a conversation one does not know beforehand what will come out of it, and one usually does not break it off unless forced to do so, because there is always something more you want to say, which is the measure of a real conversation.[4]

Why do we have to get 'caught up' in another person? Why is this so important to us? How can it improve us? In Gadamer's view a conversation cannot be ended unless we really want to stop it. This is because we always want to say everything for the sake of exploring other's views and thus the conversation persistently develops. This nature also reinforces why we are not capable of knowing what comes out of a conversation. Besides that, we cannot avoid the fact that by making conversation we obtain better insights. These new insights have transformative power even though our conversation is about something that we have experienced before. Thus, the aim of a conversation is not to look for the same standpoints or adapt two different standpoints. This means that someone cannot impel the other to have the same standpoint as him/her because a conversation does not aim to make someone follow in the other's standpoint or vice versa. Nevertheless, the truth sought in a conversation will drive

---

3. Thomas K Carr, *Newman and Gadamer: Toward Hermeneutics of Religious Knowledge* (Atlanta, Georgia: Scholars Press, 1996), 58–59.
4. Hans-Georg Gadamer in *Conversation: Reflection and Commentary,* edited and translated by Richard E Palmer (New Haven and London: Yale University Press, 2001), 59.

each participant to adopt certain acts of other participant. That is why a conversation helps to improve ourselves.

As mentioned above, to Gadamer reaching a common standpoint is not addressed by conversation, but several compromises occur. Thus, the aim of every conversation is compromise, although it becomes a debate.[5] In other words, as per Gadamer's thought, differences will lead us to compromises. The long debates in a conversation are always ended by compromises. In conversation, what we have in our mind before, will be considered again because we find new and different views from the other, which then bring us to compromise the view we held. Therefore, through conversation we will 're-define the border of our own horizon by clarifying them over against the other',[6] which in turn causes our interpretative vocabularies to widen.[7] A conversation impels us to consider the border of our horizon based on the views which are offered by others so that we enlarge our horizon and replace a new border of our horizon. In addition, a conversation broadens our interpretative vocabularies for in conversation we obtain a variety of words to describe the same subject matter, words which we have never used before.

The explanation above also makes it obvious that a clarification of understanding is possible through conversation.[8] One's truth claim which is expressed in a society, together with existing social prejudices, has the potential to initiate conflicts between peoples and groups. We need to clarify the claims and to make compromises which create a good life for all.

Gadamer's explanation of conversation as described above can make people think that truths are achieved from the end result of a conversation. In contrast to that statement, to Gadamer, truths appear or occur when the process of dialogue goes on. The last decision is not the essence of dialogue, for the essence of dialogue is 'the dialectic between statement and counterstatement'.[9] The position of language is so important that Gadamer regards conversation as a 'linguistic process, language on the

---

5. Carr, *Newman and Gadamer: Toward a Hermeneutics of Religious Knowledge*, 59.
6. *Ibid.*
7. *Ibid.*
8. Warnke, *Gadamer: Hermeneutics, Tradition, and Reason* (Cambridge: Polity Press, 1987), 100.
9. Paul Fairfield, 'Truth Without Methodologism: Gadamer and James', in *American Catholic Philosophical Quarterley*, LXVII/3, 1993: 295.

move'.[10] This view affirms Heidegger's thought that the essence of language is conversation.[11]

The power of language is shown in the process of conversation. In conversation, participants surrender themselves to the power of language and let the power lead them to the play of questioning and answering.[12]

Gadamer's views on the power of language have raised a number of issues for Ambrosio:

> We must ask what kind of power language has over us and how that power is related to truth. This in turn leads us to consider a second question, namely, how the power of language comes to rule our understanding through the play of question and answer, thereby constituting a criterion which judges the truth-value of our experience insofar as we understand.[13]

Furthermore, Ambrosio affirms that the foundation of Gadamer's hermeneutics is that truth occurs in human existence through the power of language.[14]

For Gadamer the power of language becomes visible when we begin to enter the playing field, when language opens through questions. In the language game we act as people who want to learn so that our understanding of the world is developed.[15] As a result, the power of language allows us to live in the neighborhood of truth which in turn leads us to our willingness in achieving the highest good.[16]

The idea that truth occurs when a conversation keeps on going, not before or after it, according to Habermas, is difficult to accept since it does not take into account the fact that conversation itself can be corrupt so that as a result it is not a truth, but is domination.[17] The corruption, to

---

10. Theodore Kisiel, *The Happening of Tradition: The Hermeneutics of Gadamer and Heidegger,* Edited Robert Hollinger. *Hermeneutics and Praxis* (Notre Dame, Indiana: University of Notre Dame Press, 1985), 10.

11. *Ibid.*

12. Francis J Ambrosio, 'Gadamer, Plato, and the Discipline of Dialogue', in *International Philosophical Quarterly* Vol XXVII/1/105 March 1987: 19–20.

13. *Ibid*, 26.

14. *Ibid*, 19–20.

15. *Ibid*, 29.

16. *Ibid*, 31.

17. Paul FSC Giurlanda, 'Habermas' Critique of Gadamer: Does it Stand Up?', in *International Philosophical Quarterly,* XXVII/1/105 March 1987: 35.

Habermas, is also caused by corrupt language, and as long as critical theory has not replaced its authenticity a conversation is just a utopian dream. Based on this, Habermas believes that Gadamer regards the word 'conversation' too highly.[18] In my view, in contrast to Habermas, it is not difficult to accept that truth occurs when a conversation keeps going because if we say that the truth occurs in the beginning of a conversation, the conversation becomes useless and we do not need it to continue any further. Meanwhile, it seems a conclusion if we say that the truth is obtained after a conversation. In addition, Gadamer stresses that in genuine and 'true' conversation there is no leader or follower. This means that in genuine and 'true' conversation there is no domination.

Real conversation, for Gadamer, happens when each participant focuses completely on the core of the discussion and finds truths. Real conversation is based on our own understanding, on the awareness that we are not without limitations and that we are historical beings, and on the fact that we do not have an absolute knowledge of our world. Real conversation has to focus on acquiring a powerful argument from the other participant. The goal of one's statement is not a quarrel but the possible truth.[19] It is clear that truth is gained from the core of the problem which is in dispute.[20] In other words, participants have to focus on the perspicacity of truth of a problem, neither to defend their own views nor to defeat other's.[21] To obtain this objective, certainly, several items have to be taken into consideration.

Conversation, for Gadamer, requires the two participants speak the same language.[22] Without the same language, it is impossible to attain a discerning argument with the other. Misunderstandings easily occur when each participant is incapable of understanding the other.

Conversation also requires the two participants be open to each other and acknowledge the value of the other's thoughts. 'Reaching an understanding in conversation presupposes that both partners are ready for it and are trying to recognise the full value of what is alien and opposed to them.'[23] This means that a participant does not perceive that s/he has a

---

18. *Ibid.*
19. Warnke, *Gadamer: Hermeneutics, Tradition, and Reason,* 100.
20. *Ibid,* 102.
21. Paul Healy, 'Situated Rationality and Hermeneutics Understanding: A Gadamerian Approach to Rationality', in *International Philosophical Quarterly,* XXXVI/2/142 June 1996: 169.
22. Gadamer, *Truth and Method,* 347.
23. *Ibid,* 348.

more valuable insight than the other and does not state that a discovery is his/her own exclusively.[24] To have such convictions, however, participants have to listen to each other, not just hear the other's words.[25] Each participant has to appreciate and listen prudently to the other's argument as his/her own argument. In addition, these requirements have to be recognised and acknowledged by both participants, as they convey their own particular arguments. The participants also have to be aware that arguments can be approved or rejected by the other participant. What one assumes as the truth maybe in accordance with the other's form (assumptions) of the truth, but it can also take on a different—even opposing—form, meaning that one of the participants insists that the truth is solely his/hers alone. Nevertheless, Gadamer emphasises that people will agree on many things. This is because the limitation of reasoning brings an inevitable consequence, which is that people hold on to common prepositions.[26]

The achieved truth, according to Gadamer, can be attested through an agreement, not through a trial that the agreement is covered or uncovered. This thought is to counter Habermas' objection that Gadamer needed to realise that manipulation can be involved in an agreement. Moreover, Gadamer asserts that an 'agreement' resulted by manipulation cannot be called an agreement. What Habermas referred to as manipulated agreement is like a process of offering in a contract where those who make a contract, sometimes or even usually, do not have the same position. The stronger side oppresses or controls the other weaker side. Therefore, an agreement which occurs is not a real agreement.

Gadamer realised that whatever requirements are fulfilled in a conversation, genuine dialogue is still difficult. This is because the resulted truth in a conversation depends much more on each participant's sincerity.

The Significance of Openness

As mentioned before, a conversation requires openness, and is a characteristic of every true conversation. Gadamer describes openness as follows:

---

24. Kisiel, 'The Happening of Tradition: The Hermeneutics of Gadamer and Heidegger', 10.
25. Richard E Palmer, *Gadamer in Conversation: Reflections and Commentary* (New Heaven & London: Yale University Press, 2001), 39.
26. WSK Cameron, 'On Communicative Actors Talking Past One Another: The Gadamer-Habermas Debate', in *Philosophy Today,* Spring, 1996: 163.

Thus it is characteristic of every true conversation that each
opens himself to the other person, truly accepts his points
of view as worthy of consideration and gets inside the other
to such an extent that he understands not a particular individual, but what he says. The thing that has to be grasped is
the objective rightness or otherwise of his opinion, so that
they can agree with each other on the subject. Thus the other
not relate to other's opinion to him, but to one's own views.[27]

Openness is not only the ability to view the other's argument as valuable but also to cause someone to reconsider his/her own arguments. The
stronger partner's argument which can provide obvious evidence will shift
someone's insight, and makes him/her realise that the other's argument
is more proficient than his/her, or vice versa. However, compromise in
regard to a problem, broadens each participant's insights without seeing
whether his/her argument is stronger or weaker than the other's. This can
only happen if participants focus on what is said without noticing who
said it. By doing this, participants will be capable of finding relevance so
that an agreement is reached.

This description shows that openness in dialogue is obligatory.
Accordingly, if participants engage in a dialogue without being willing
to open themselves, a true dialogue can never occur. In addition, for
Gadamer, openness is a requirement that is more important than
methodological consideration in approaching the topic. However, for
Gadamer, the significance of openness is essential in a dialogue as Hogan
points out:

One can never come to a dialogue with his mind made up.
Openness on both sides is essential. Neither pole can control. Rather than engaging in a dialogue, Gadamer tells us, it
engages us. In this manner it can be seen that the outcome
of the dialogue can never be known in advance. A genuine
dialogue is a process in which the give and take assists the
participants in arriving at a new understanding.[28]

---

27. Gadamer, *Truth and Method*, 347.
28. John P Hogan, 'Gadamer and the Hermeneutical Experience', in *Philosophy Today*, 20
    1976: 7.

Openness brings consequences which are needed by conversation, namely, no one can control the direction of the conversation, and participants are merely involved and do not know the result of the conversation. This does not mean that we cannot presume the result but we have to be ready to accept that the result is far from our presumption. The certain result of conversation is that each participant comes to a new understanding.

Gadamer states that openness in dialogue has two meanings: (1) openness to learn, and (2) openness to respond. The former emphasises that someone wants to learn from and be open to another person's horizon. This only occurs if someone considers the other person's horizon as being valuable. The latter means that someone wants to prudently respond to the other. Learning from and being open to another person's horizon drives one to respond to it, and people will, hopefully, reconsider their own opinion, thus leading to greater understanding. Therefore, openness is the characteristic of self correction and understanding.

Nevertheless, according to Gadamer, there are people who do not have a horizon:

> The horizon is the range of vision that includes everything that can be seen from a particular vantage point . . .
>
> A person who has no horizon is a man who does not see far enough and hence overvalues what is nearest to him. Contrariwise, to have a horizon means not to be limited to what is nearest, but to be able to see beyond it. A person who has a horizon knows the relative significance of everything within this horizon, as near or far, great or small.[29]

This asserts that there are people who do not possess a horizon, namely those who cannot see far enough. The problem is what if a person is involved in a conversation, and at the time of dialogue that person wanted to know their horizon, or were questioned by the other about their horizon and it was clear that they did not have one? Or, is it that everyone does have their own respective horizon, whether it be in different sizes, some wide and others narrow? Unfortunately, Gadamer does not discuss the matter while he states that we fall into conversation and during the conversation we strive to know and understand the other's horizon.

---

29. Gadamer, *Truth and Method*, 269.

Gadamer believes that to become a person with a horizon is not without effort because it stems from 'hard-earned result'[30] of an experience. All experiences are open to be explored, but it depends on a person's ability to learn from their experiences or not. If they can truly grasp the meaning of an experience by opening themselves to its possibilities, then they will broaden their horizons. That is why Gadamer thinks that openness has one of the defining structures of experience.

In a true conversation, participants will know the other person's horizon, but if participants only know the other person's horizon for the sake of arriving at an agreement, it cannot be regarded as a genuine conversation.

> The same is true of a conversation that we have with someone simply in order to get to know him ie to discover his standpoint and his horizon. This is not true conversation, in the sense that we not seeking agreement concerning an object, but the specific contents of the conversation are only a means to get to know the horizon of the other person.[31]

Furthermore, Gadamer states that knowing the other person's horizon does not mean that we have to necessarily agree with it, but it drives us to intelligible ideas. We are capable of viewing something in proper and good proportion.[32] In addition, we can place ourselves in the other person's situation so that it appears as an *awareness of otherness*.

In spite of knowing the other person's horizon, in conversation, there is a fusion of horizon which occurs. When the fusion of horizon occurs, each participant no longer cares with his/her own or the other's opinion. In other words, participants do not differentiate or defend their own opinion. This means that they will broaden their own horizon and realise that the other has something that makes them know more.

The explanation above affirms that true conversation is difficult because openness, as its characteristic, cannot be clearly measured. A person's openness can only can be known definitely by his/her ownself. Again,

---

30. Cameron, 'On Communicative Actors Talking Past One Another: The Gadamer-Habermas Debate', 163.
31. Hans-Georg Gadamer, 'The Historicity of Understanding'. Kurt Mueller Volmer. *The Hermeneutics Reader: Texts of the German Tradition from Enlightenment to the* Present (New York: Continuum, 1985), 270.
32. Gadamer, *Truth and Method*, 272.

a true conversation occurs depending on the sincerity of the participants in the conversation.

Question and Answer

Another thing necessary to pay attention to in relation to Gadamer's thought of dialogue is his logic of question and answer. In his book *Truth and Method* Gadamer discusses the dynamics of question and answer in a passage titled *the logic of question and answer*.[33] According to Gadamer, the logic of question and answer is the logic of discovery in terms of people coming to understanding. In the logic of question and answer, people try to find understanding about their subjects through discussion or speaking.

Gadamer places the logic and question in important positions such as *more fundamental criterion of truth* and *the constitutive way of understanding*.[34] Certainly, this thought needs critical explanation, and the following discussion addresses the matter at hand.

In conversation, question and answer occur in reciprocal relation. The dialectic of question and answer can only occur if participants create 'friendly discussion'.[35] Each participant creates a pleasant condition because the dialogue conducted is to obtain goodness for all, namely to find the good in human life. In other words, dialogue is for our own interest in creating good life. 'Friendly discussion' can be created because participants listen to each other and believe that the other opinion is valuable. A participant has to consider the partner as a friend who also wants to contribute his/her valuable insights for human life, not to regard him/her as an opponent who wants to attack the other views for the sake of demonstrating that s/he has more valuable views than the other.

The dialectics of question and answer, for Gadamer, warrants truth but does not guarantee it. An agreement created in conversation could reinforce truth, but it is understood that the truth is still possible, meaning that it is possible if one day, strong arguments appear to replace the truth. Here, Aristotle assists Gadamer's thought in stressing that the logical rule

---

33. *Ibid*, 333–341.
34. Ambrosio, 'Gadamer, Plato, and the Discipline of Dialogue', 17 and 18.
35. Lawrence, 'Gadamer and Lonergan: A Dialectical Comparison', in *International Philosophical Quarterly*, 20, 1980: 35.

of question and answer reinforces people to pass uncertainty and universal openness (question) to certainty and concreteness (answer).[36]

From the dialectics of question and answer, we expect to reach the truth. Accordingly, in conversation, participants examine their prejudices and each of them has to play by the rules in order to become cooperative in achieving the truth.[37]

The prejudices which are challenged in this manner bring people to understanding.[38] A participant realises that there are other prejudices related to a subject matter as the partner conveys their ideas. To make these prejudices reach the truth, participants need to come to the affair of questioning and answering in an open manner. Thus, understanding is the event of the encounter between question and answer.[39] This thought affirms Bacon, Descartes and Collingwood's thoughts. Bacon and Descartes believe that knowledge is achieved through the process of question and answer. Therefore, the questions have to be true and asked in the proper order.[40] Meanwhile, Collingwood states that understanding is a product of the dialectics of question and answer which is always open and beyond the inquirer's control. In Collingwood's view, knowledge is obtained from the continuous process of questioning. This condition shows that the process of question and answer is influenced by history, that something wrong is replaced by truth but it is still open to be replaced by something new. Accordingly, he believes that the past is telescoped into the present and the relation of question and answer is the process of being 'prospectively open but retrospectively determinate'.[41] Still, in line with Collingwood, Gadamer also shows that there is a relation between question and history. This is why Hogan states that Gadamer is indebted to Collingwood who demonstrates how history is not only the past, but a past which is formulated in the awareness of historians.[42] Based on this,

36. Ambrosio, 'Gadamer and Aristotle: Hermeneutics as Participant in Tradition', in *Hermeneutic and the Tradition*, edited by Daniel O Dahlstrom (Washington: The American Catholic Philosophical Association, 1988), 175.

37. Hans-Georg Gadamer, 'On the Circle of Understanding', in *Hermeneutics Versus Science? Three German Views*, edited and translated by John M Connolly and Thomas Keutner (Notre Dame, Indiana: University of Notre Dame Press, 1988), 77–78.

38. Healy, 'Situated Rationality and Hermeneutics Understanding: a Gadamerian Approach to Rationality', 162.

39. Hogan, 'Gadamer and the Hermeneutical Experience', 9.

40. John Hogan 'Hermeneutics and The Logic of Question and Answer: Collingwood and Gadamer', in *Heythrop Journal* XXVIII 1987: 266.

41. Mink as quoted by Hogan, *ibid*, 267.

42. Hogan, *ibid*, 272.

a person has to reconstruct questions from his/her historical act which leads to answers.

Different to the general views, for Gadamer, a question has a significant function because it concerns human knowledge and openness. A conversation, according to Gadamer, can be seen from perspective of 'the suddenness of question' which opens our thoughts and allows a response.[43] Besides that, knowledge can only be attained from people who have questions.[44] The questions lead people to openness because people cannot actually experience something unless they ask questions.[45] Moreover, he believes that truth is revealed more through questions than through responses to the questions which he calls 'the logical priority of the question'.[46] Truth belongs to the question and questioning, while the answer has validity.[47] This is in line with Collingwood's thought, namely something is seen to be true or not true only after someone understands the questions which are addressed in the answers. This is a bit different to Gadamer who believes that truth is more in the question than the answer. Collingwood states that truth belongs to 'a question and answer complex', not in a preposition or a number of preposition.[48]

Following Plato and Socrates' ideas, Gadamer considers that it is more difficult for people to ask a question than to answer it. A question requires new knowledge, and this depends on participants being in dialogue in terms that participants have the desire to know a potential truth of question and truly realise that which they do not know.

Gadamer also adopts Plato view on dialogue concerning two kinds of discourses: false and genuine. False discourse is indicated by a partner who believes that his/her own thought is true. Dialogue is done to prove that the person himself is true, not to search for new knowledge. Such discourse will cause the question to seem to be easier than the answer, but actually, s/he cannot ask a true question. A genuine discourse is a discourse which truly conveys knowledge of an object. Accordingly, the essence of the question, according to Gadamer, is ' . . . the opening up, and keeping open, of possibilities'[49] or ' . . . to open up possibilities and keep them

---

43. *Ibid*, 271.
44. Gadamer, *Truth and Method*, 325.
45. *Ibid*.
46. Ambrosio, 'Gadamer and Aristotle: Hermeneutics as Participant in Tradition', 179.
47. Ambrosio, 'Gadamer, Plato, and the Discipline of Dialogue', 19.
48. Hogan, 'Hermeneutics and The Logic of Question and Answer: Collingwood and Gadamer', 9.
49. Gadamer, *Truth and Method*, 266.

open'.[50] Thus, a question is a place to prove possibilities. In other words, questioning opens the possibilities of meaning. Therefore, every question opens terms of uncertainty. This openness naturally brings positive and negative considerations. It means that knowledge which is brought up by questioning can be considered not only as something correct but also as something wrong. This openness does not mean that questioning is limited because it is limited by the horizon of questioning. The limitation of the questioning horizon leads humans to realise that they are not without limitation.[51] This also proves the limitation of human reason in finding a true question. Gadamer emphasises that people who ask questions have to be able to maintain the orientation of openness in terms of continuously asking questions.[52]

Concerning the orientation of openness, Gadamer asserts that questioning has its own art, namely the ability to continuously ask questions which is also called the art of thinking and leads to dialectics because it conducts true conversation. The art of conversation requires two people, meaning a partner who is considerate of our thoughts and does not refuse to consider them.[53]

In daily life, according to Gadamer, we find many distorted questions. Gadamer uses the word 'distortion' to show that there are questions behind the question but they do not lead in the right direction because the right questions clearly lead us to certainty.[54] This is in line with Collingwood's thought of 'right' questions where there question which do not go in the 'right' direction and which cause an impossible answer.[55] According to him, a detailed and specific answer is given when there is a detailed and specific question, and a person will not know the meaning of a preposition if the question does not address an answer.

A question, for Gadamer, makes us learn new experiences and 'right' opinion and this is a continuous process.[56] Therefore, in a genuine conversation, a question is addressed in an answer and the answer then becomes

50. Hans-Georg Gadamer in *Hermeneutics Versus Science? Three German Views*, 77.
51. Hogan, 'Hermeneutics and the Logic of Question and Answer', 271.
52. Gadamer, *Truth and Method*, 330.
53. *Ibid.*
54. Hogan, 'Hermeneutics and the Logic of Question and Answer: Collingwood and Gadamer', 266.
55. *Ibid.*
56. Healy, 'Situated Rationality and Hermeneutics Understanding: A Gadamerian Approach to Rationality', 167.

a basis of the next question, which finally leads to an agreement or a disagreement.[57]

Thus, according to Gadamer, dialogue aims to understand truth. Truth for each person in the dialogue, but it should still be realised that the truth is shared by all, 'the truth of being in question'.[58] However there are times when Gadamer does not provide sufficient explanation of what he means by the discipline of questioning and answering, as noted by Ambrosio. As a result, the thought which is offered in *Truth and Method* does not really solve our problem of understanding this today.[59] What we can learn from Gadamer's logic of question and answer is how truth and the freedom to know belong together in human existence.

Although there are still several debatable ideas of Gadamer's discipline of dialogue, this does not mean that it does not make an important contribution. In the next chapter, we will see this kind of dialogue based on human finitude as applied to interreligious dialogue and view its contributions.

---

57. Ambrosio, 'Gadamer, Plato, and the Discipline of Dialogue', 29.
58. *Ibid*, 32.
59. *Ibid*, 19.

Relating Gadamer's Concept of Finitude to Interreligious Dialogue

Gadamer was not a philosopher with a large concern for religious issues. Hence, when he discussed human finitude and proposed a model of dialogue, he did not relate these ideas to religion or religious dialogue. Nevertheless, I believe that his ideas on human finitude, with its emphasis on the importance of the 'awareness of otherness' makes an enormous contribution to religious issues especially to the area of interreligious dialogue. Therefore in this chapter, I analyse Gadamer's ideas in relation to interreligious dialogue. To assist in that endeavour I will also use Knitter's four models of examining interreligious dialogue and so begin by outlining these models.

The Replacement Model

For Knitter, people who take the replacement model of dialogue in interreligous dialogue base their conviction on the claim that what God wants and humans need only one religion.[1] They believe that humans truly need such a center and they provide social and geopolitical reasons for this certainty. For instance, the problems faced by human beings today such as war, violence, famine, implore upon humans to overcome these issues together. In other words, like a family we act together for the sake of finding the solution for the problems that are faced by the family.

---

1. Paul F Knitter, *Introducing Theologies of Religions* (Maryknoll, NY: Orbis Books, 2002), 19.

Thus, people who prefer this model want to remind everybody that there is a human problem that really exists: there is something wrong with humanity and the world and that is reflected in the use of terms such as 'original sin', 'suffering', 'ignorance', 'forgetfulness', or 'imbalance'. But, due to their limitation, humans cannot solve the problems surrounding them by themselves. Therefore, they need a 'Higher Power' to help them to find the solution. They believe that the solution is one not many solutions, and one religion and not many religions: their own religion.[2]

Perhaps, the statement that 'God wants and humans need only one religion' leads people to think that this model intends to do away with diversity, but what this model tries to achieve is to unite it, as explained in the following passage by Knitter:

> That does not mean removing diversity; but it does require binding the diversity in a newly won unity. For this to be possible, it makes evident, again, that if there is a God, this God would provide the one criterion of truth, the one center of unity that can connect, and then hold, people together. But this isn't easy, mainly because there is always one nation, or people, that sets itself above all the others as the master-builder of unity. This, too, Newbigin tells us, is the reason we need not just 'one truth' but 'one God-given truth'.[3]

We have to overcome the problems around us together and thus need a center, but such a center, if we link this to Gadamer's thought, is unacceptable because the center that we need does not come from one religion but from compromises of many people who have different backgrounds in terms of culture, religion, social status, etc. From Gadamer's perspective, the idea that people do not want to remove diversity but to bind it in 'a newly won unity' is impossible. In addition, it is not a unity because it merely offers one 'true' religion.

People in this model assert that although God's love is universal, it is offered through a specific and singular community. They also emphasise that we cannot say that the final truth does not exist simply because we cannot find them without difficulties. This claim causes people to have an extreme point of view, as Knitter points out:

---

2. *Ibid.*
3. *Ibid*, 30–31.

> They feel that it really allows for no value, no presence of God, in other religions, viewing them as entirely man-made, as obstacles to, rather than conduits for, God's love. In theological terms, there is neither revelation nor salvation in the world of other religions.[4]

This is the reason why other religions have to be replaced by the 'one' true religion. However, people who follow this model allow the followers of other religions to make the same statement that their religion is also the only true religion. There is a tolerance of other world religions.

Returning to Gadamer, he agrees that universal truths exist but believes that they are hard to achieve. Nevertheless, according to Gadamer, we should not say that universal truths are ours or belong to a specific and singular community and thus, by extension, to one world religion. Moreover, this idea also seems to eradicate human finitude, that is that what people hold as valued is influenced by their respective tradition, experience and language. For Gadamer, we cannot impel other people to have the same opinions that we have. This does not mean that we cannot conduct dialogue with people who have an opinion that the universal truth are theirs alone or belong to their community because it is inevitable that every person has his/her own claim of truth and prejudice. Moreover, prejudice does not limit human effort in seeking truths. This is also the reason that we need to have dialogue between people. Through dialogue, clarification and understanding is possible.

Based on this conviction the replacement model of interreligious dialogue is a 'holy competition', meaning different religions compete with each other to prove that they truly have the ultimate and universal truth. In addition, this competition is ideally peaceful, sincere, open, honest, nonviolent, natural, necessary and helpful. According to Knitter, in this model, we can find people who want to learn from and listen respectfully to the followers of other religions, but they believe that their own religion will come out to be the winner in any discussion.[5]

From Gadamer's point of view, although dialogue occurs, there is something 'bothering' in this model, that is, each participant aims to defend his/her own opinion, and at the end of the dialogue s/he wants the others to acknowledge that s/he has the universal truth by which they have to follow him/her. According to Gadamer, we are actually allowed to

---

4. *Ibid*, 33.
5. *Ibid*, 31.

have our own 'truth', but it is better to postpone it or to regard it as possible truth until we have an understanding through dialogue. In addition, people who have the awareness of limitation acknowledge that they do not have the absolute knowledge of the world.

There are two kinds replacement model, total replacement as described above and also partial replacement. In partial replacement, people believe that God speaks to all human beings, 'God voice is heard *within*, from movements of heart and through events of history'.[6] Pannenberg defines the history of religion as 'the history of the appearing of the Divine Mystery which is presupposed in the structure of human existence'.[7] When one applies Pannenberg's view to this model it does not mean that all religions lead people to salvation, because the revelation of other religions is inadequate to drive the followers to salvation.[8] While other religions always try to win God's way of salvation, there is at the same time a belief that the one true religion is God's one and only way of salvation.[9]

From the explanation above, this model of dialogue is based on the desire to invite the followers of other religions to follow God's way of salvation. Sharing of information between each religion occurs, mainly addressed to correct each other to explain why the other religions convictions are false. Therefore, the nature of this model is evangelistic without disrespecting others religious beliefs. For Netland, this kind of dialogue leads people to do away with the venom of prejudice, mistrust and conflict among the followers of different religions. Moreover, this model convinces people that 'if conversation with others is carried out in this way, and if everyone really listens and opens their hearts . . . people really hear and find God'.[10]

The nature of this model brings out the fact that 'there are going to be many more differences than similarities'.[11] For Pannenberg, 'It is precisely the conflictual positions and truth claims of the religions that have to become the subject of dialogue'.[12]

In contrast, Gadamer emphasises that there will be agreement because we share common human experiences as well as common human prob-

---

6. *Ibid*, 35.
7. Wolfhart Pannenberg, *Basic Question in Theology*, (Philadelphia, Fortress, 1971), 112.
8. Knitter, *Introducing Theologies of Religions*, 36.
9. *Ibid*, 39.
10. *Ibid*, 41.
11. *Ibid*.
12. Wolfhart Pannenberg, 'The Religions from the Perspective of Christian Theology', in *Modern Theology* 9, 1993: 286–287.

lems. Therefore, we should not only emphasise differences of the subject of the dialogue, but also its similarities.

Thus, in this partial replacement model, the dialogue is still viewed as a 'holy competition'. One religion endeavours to prove itself 'superior in illuminating the people's experience of their life and world',[13] meaning 'superior in answering the innermost questions and needs of the human heart and the needs of our messed-up, selfish, violent world'.[14] Accordingly, the characteristics of dialogue in this model are persuading, inviting and attracting. In addition, ' . . . this dialogical competition must always be carried out with genuine respect for the dignity, intelligence, and religious freedom of the other believers'.[15]

As aforementioned, for Gadamer the claim that someone has the universal truth is actually allowed but it is better to postpone it until s/he obtains an adequate understanding of the other through dialogue. From the description above, people who are part of this model do strive to prove that their own claim of truth is 'the truth' by holding on to that claim at the beginning of a dialogue and making it the aim of the dialogue. Besides that, there are several questions which arise in relation to this model: Can they avoid what Gadamer calls a 'distorted question', a question which leads them clearly, to find the weakness of others' thoughts? Given human finitude, can people who follow this model realise that their opinion is also influenced by their backgrounds of tradition, language, experience, culture and other conditions? Do they realise that they use, following Knitter's term, one of the 'telescopes' in viewing what they believe and it is really possible that others use other telescopes?

In summary, from Gadamer's point of view it is better for people who take follow model to realise that one's understanding of the world is really limited in any tradition, language and experience, and this is the case for every person. This awareness truly helps us in our encounter with others between those who have different or even contradictory truth claims. This awareness also makes people be very careful in viewing other religions, as Knitter has also noted regarding this model.

Finally, although Gadamer's model of dialogue actually allows participants to have truth claims, the dialogue is not a competition where each participant defends her/his truth claim and tries to invite others to have

---

13. *Ibid.*
14. Knitter, *Introducing Theologies of Religions,* 41.
15. *Ibid.*

the same claim of truth, but it is a compromise or following Knitter's term, is always cooperation.

The Fulfillment Model

The followers of the fulfillment model, according to Knitter, want to create balance between the universality and the particularity of God's love. The conviction that God wants to save all the people becomes the background of this model. Hence, value can be found in other religions, thus dialogue is needed and there is even salvation in other religions. As Catholic theologian Karl Rahner argues God allows human beings to have diversity of life and action.[16] Rahner emphasises that the followers of other religions can truly find God and this is because God shows His presence and love through every human being's nature. In other words, human nature is that they are capable of feeling the presence of 'Infinite Being' although they are 'finite beings'.[17]

The idea is similar to Gadamer's thought of openness, that is, that people have to regard that the opinions other others have are of equal value to their own opinion. The background to this model also shows that people who follow this model realise that human finitude is an inevitable fact of life, thus there is diversity, and there is no willingness to bind all of life into one.

Rahner outlines the first area we have to explore if we consider that God performs throughout human history and if we think that this has to be noticeable and be a form of religion. Accordingly, religions can be regarded as 'ways of salvation' and other religions can be 'a positive means of gaining the right relationship to God and thus for the attaining of salvation, a means which is therefore positively included in God's plan of salvation'.[18] Nevertheless, Rahner emphasises that although the followers of other religions are able to experience God's love, they have not had a clear view yet whether the experience leads them to the true purposes and possibilities or not. Thus, people who take this model still regard their own religion as having 'a . . . greater chance for salvation'.[19]

To regard that we are superior to others and we believe that other people cannot fully achieve a good life is indeed uncomfortable for the other,

---

16. Karl Rahner as quoted by Knitter in *Introducing Theologies of Religions*, 69.

17. *Ibid.*

18. *Ibid*, 71.

19. *Ibid*, 73.

but this thought, from Gadamer's perspective, is allowed as long as we can postpone it or regard it as a prejudice which needs to be proven through dialogue. In addition, dialogue is not addressed to reinforce our own truth claim. If the followers of this model want to reinforce their own truth claim, they will repeat what the replacement model does: failing to avoid distorted questions. They will make questions which clearly lead the others to give an answer as they hope.

Still in line with Rahner, D'Costa states that we will value, listen to as well as learn from other religions if we accept that there is the presence of God in other religions. Nevertheless, what is learned from the other is addressed to help us understand our own religion. In other words, we capture the advantages of the others for the sake of cleaning our own religion from 'distortion'.

Listening to and learning from others is emphasised by Gadamer because it leads people to be more open to others which in turn makes people redefine their own horizon. From listening to and learning from others, the fusion of horizon occurs, and for Gadamer, people will not care anymore about their own thoughts. This indication is not found in this model because their aim is to invite the other to have the same belief.

From the ideas above, the dialogue offered is still considered as a holy competition although openness is more evident compared to the commitment. This is because the message attained from the dialogue is addressed to reinforce the understanding and knowledge of our own religion.

According to Gadamer, dialogue is not addressed to support our own opinions. In contrast, dialogue makes us reexamine and review our own opinions. The questions in dialogue are really addressed to lead participants to a better insight, thus the clarification of our understanding occurs. Therefore, after engaging in a conversation, each participant will improve themselves. However, how does dialogue occur if each participant aims to reinforce their own truth?

The Mutuality Model

The mutuality model, as Knitter has outlined it, focuses more on God's universal love and presence in other religions. It aims to answer three questions related to a more authentic dialogue, a level playing field for dialogue and a clearer understanding of religion's uniqueness which keeps the dialogue going.[20]

People who take this model not only realise the diversity of religions but also regard the followers of other religions as 'potential dialogue partners'.[21] They regard relationship in terms of dialogue as more significant than diversity or plurality. This is the reason that this model is called mutuality model rather than the pluralism model.

Similar to the mutuality model, Gadamer puts dialogue in a significant position: the essence of human understanding and the act of self-correcting. This means that dialogue compels people to have the ability to understand something including other people's views. In addition, through dialogue, our horizon is wider than before and this makes us have better insight.

To build the relationship, a level playing field for dialogue is needed where all religions have the same rights in both speaking about their religious values and listening to other's. Therefore, in this model, the claim that one religion as being something God-given is avoided since it leads the believers to claim that their religion holds the absolute truth and it would also lead them to see other religions as inferior. This model maintains diversity and indeed views it as the reason to engage in conversation between believers.[22] Hence, people have to avoid the idea which states that all religions truthfully talk about the same thing, but they have to realise that religions have something in common, which is an inevitable fact and, even that fact alone, would make dialogue possible.[23] The diversity which transforms to uniqueness in each religion has to be re-evaluated and re-examined based on new experience resulting from conversation. What is also required is a new understanding of uniqueness that leads people to be open to other religions.[24]

From Gadamer's perspective, this description shows that the followers of this model realise the fact of human finitude so that they maintain diversity and open themselves, and not just hear but really listen to the partners. They also understand openness appropriately, namely that they regard others' opinions have the same value as their own. Gadamer also believes that humans will agree on many things because human reason-

---

20. *Ibid*, 109–112.
21. *Ibid*, 110.
22. *Ibid*.
23. *Ibid*, 111.
24. *Ibid*.

ing is limited. This implies that although there is diversity, there are many similarities as well, and diversity can always be compromised. Meanwhile, re-evaluating and re-examining diversity would broaden our horizons and our vocabularies which in turn leads us to re-define our previous understanding of others.

Nevertheless, from Gadamer's perspective, people do not need to avoid the claim that their religion is the only true religion. However, all religions have their own truth claims. In addition, we are actually allowed to have prejudices towards the others, and through dialogue we examine our prejudices so that we obtain legitimate prejudices. Thus, what we need is to adjourn our opinions and truth claims.

This model provides three bridges which enable people to choose the mutuality model of dialogue that is the philosophical-historical bridge, the mystical bridge and the ethical-practical bridge. Based on the philosophical-historical point of view, religions seem to use different languages, various directions and no common goal for them thus they play numerous games. In fact human history shows that all religions have 'holy people' who brought the teaching of how to live in the world in terms of live in peace with the others.[25] This means that all religions have a common goal but because it is expressed in a variety of words some people assume that religions have different languages.

In line with the philosophical bridge, Gadamer provides the reason humans have various languages. He states that human words are various because of human reason. Human reasoning is limited in describing something through language. As a result, human language limits humans' understanding.

As Knitter says, Hick who sustains this model states that all religious traditions are 'both ancient and widespread'[26] and they differentiate between the Godhead, that is beyond human experience, and that which is limited, humanity. Hence, for Hick, experience is always 'experiencing as'[27] meaning that what we know about an object is but an image of it or 'thing's *phenomenon*',[28] we never achieve an exact knowledge of an object or the noumenon. Hick emphasises that humans should realise that their specific historical, social and psychological life truthfully enables them

---

25. *Ibid*, 115.
26. Knitter, *Introducing Theologies of Religions*, 115. See John Hicks, *Problems of Religious Pluralism* (London: Macmillan, 1985), 28–45.
27. John Hick, *Problems of Religious Pluralism*, 17, 27 122.
28. Knitter, *Introducing Theologies of Religions*, 116.

to form their experience of God. He continues that ethical area is more workable than doctrinal one in avoiding the trap of relativism.[29]

Hick's ideas reinforce Gadamer's thought of human finitude. Certain social conditions, traditions, and historical backgrounds indeed influence human understanding, including human's religious understanding. As Gadamer mentions, humans cannot escape from the prejudice of their time hence a perfect understanding is never achieved, what can be done is reached, as has been the practice throughout human history, and humans try to get closer to perfect understanding.

Hick does not intend to change the religious language of uniqueness but he wants us to comprehend the language we are using. He asserts that 'one and only' language stops dialogue and offends the followers of other religions. Therefore, the fact that human knowledge is conditioned by history means a religion cannot claim that it has the absolute and full truth.

There are similarities between Hick and Gadamer. Gadamer emphasises that humans should not claim to have an absolute truth, what is said as truth is better to be regarded as possible truth. In addition, they are indeed influenced by the past. Nevertheless, from Gadamer's point of view, 'one and only' language does not stop dialogue. Such language is allowed but we have to suspend it, thus we can truly learn from and listen to others.

The mystical bridge discusses much more about the infinity, 'the same Divine Mystery or Reality is being experienced within the many different religions'.[30] This bridge also stresses that the existence of 'a core mystical experience' proves that of 'a core Mystical Reality'.[31]

The mystical bridge shows that people who are aware of their own mystical experiences cannot be limited in their own religion and this drives them to be open and sensitive in acknowledging the same mystery in other religions. The bridge stresses that 'experience tells us something real about the world and about ourselves'.[32]

Gadamer believes that experience brings us to open ourselves to the world by asking questions and this leads us to understand our world and who we are. Experience, for Gadamer, leads humans to understand reality,

---

29. *Ibid*, 119, S Mark Heim *Salvations: Truth and Difference in Religions* (Maryknoll, NY: Orbis Book, 1995), 43. See Hick, *Interpretation of Religion: Human Responses to the Transcendent* (New Haven and London: Yale University Press, 1989), 13–14, 89, 299, and 325.

30. Knitter, *Introducing Theologies of Religions*, 119.

31. *Ibid*, 126.

32. *Ibid*, 127.

and because we share a common experience, we will agree with more than we do not. Although, Gadamer believes that experience makes human understand reality better, it however cannot guarantee that people who have the same experience will have the same opinions.

This bridge also shows that mystics make us realise that the form of the Divine is not important but we know that 'the Divine breathes within the human and the material', and that if we are not aware of this, we will neither know ourselves nor the earth as well. Moreover, if we are unable to recognise the earth's 'sacredness' and 'openness', we will never understand it precisely.[33]

For Gadamer, the final understanding never exists because our understanding really depends on our finitude. But, this fact does not lead humans to be pessimistic; on the contrary humans have to be optimistic meaning that they have to be creative in finding a better understanding of themselves and the world. In addition, human experience drives them to obtain a better understanding. Gadamer stresses that an experienced person does not mean one who knows a lot of things but one who is aware of his/her limitation. This means that although we are aware of the divine, we will not attain perfect understanding of the world. In addition, due to our limitations, although people are aware of the divine, they can have different or even contrasting beliefs in relation to the divine.

Other support for this model comes from Pannikar. According to Pannikar, the fact of plurality and diversity in human life cannot be united into one, as Knitter has written:

> The religions are like the pieces of different puzzles—you're never going to be able to put them together into a pretty picture or final system. To expand this point, Panikar turns to the language of postmodernism: 'we must accept that some religious traditions are mutually incommensurable.' That means that you cannot measure one by the other, or all of them by a common yardstick. If there's any unity within the world of religions, it's surrounded and protected by a wall of diversity. You can't find the unity without diversity.[34]

---

33. *Ibid.*
34. *Ibid,* 129.

Thus, a universal system is denied and that the divine itself is also various.[35] The diversity, however, can never be the one or conclusive.[36] Based on his mystical awareness, Pannikar believes that the diversity of the divine as shown in many religions does not lead us to go into isolation to avoid the other but, on the contrary, the possibility and the need to connect with each other is clear because he believes that there is one spirit who creates the manyness and who lives within it.[37]

For Knitter, Pannikar illustrates dialogue as 'dancing together'. This means that on the one hand, all religious traditions dance together in dialogue and develop in both 'differences and togetherness', and on the other, incommensurable religious experiences enables people to be open to and learn from each other.[38] From this model of dialogue, unity is possible but it is always unfinished and imperfect.

As previously mentioned, Gadamer emphasises that diversity cannot be one because it is the inevitable fact of human finitude. What we need is not to unite it but to create a dialogue so that humans can compromise about a good life. Gadamer's thought of dialogue is in line with Pannikar's thought of dialogue. Gadamer's characteristics of dialogue can be found in Pannikar's model such as openness and learning from each other. While Pannikar states that unity may occur only in imperfect forms, Gadamer holds that unity is not the goal of dialogue. However, in contrast with Pannikar, who believes that we can connect with each other because there is one spirit who creates the manyness and lives within it, Gadamer views that the need for dialogue among humans is really needed in order to understand each other, and to clarify prejudices. Thus, we do not need to find a common ground as the reason to create dialogue.

If the mystical bridge emphasises human experiences of the same divine, the ethical-practical bridge focuses on something in common. The term which is used in this bridge is 'global responsibility'[39] in terms of suffering, poverty, famine, violence, etc. We can find all these terms in religion traditions for they all strive to overcome these ethical problems, and if there is religion which does not focus on this, it will be irrelevant and unexciting because it has lost its validity.[40] Thomas Berry reinforces this

---

35. *Ibid.*
36. *Ibid,* 130
37. *Ibid.*
38. *Ibid.*
39. *Ibid,* 134.
40. *Ibid,* 138.

idea: 'concern for wellbeing of the planet is the one concern that hopefully will bring the nations (and the religions) of the world into an inter-nation (and interreligious) community'.[41]

Based on the ethical-practical approach, the followers of different religions are being called upon to dialogue and are trying to find global ethics related to dignity, integrity, responsibility, justice, etc. Talking about eco-human suffering and acting together for the sake of overcoming it drives the dialogue to be more effective and successful. Such dialogue will lead the followers of different religions to share their perspective of faith which in turn brings them to search for an encountering at the level of faith. In addition, the participants of dialogue realise that a certain religion may have an excellent value in providing the solution of eco-human suffering.[42] Therefore, the nature of dialogue is 'the dialogue of life and struggle' where followers of one religion will view the other followers of another religion as 'real co-workers'.[43]

This idea is similar to the aim of conversation in Gadamer's thought: compromise. The diversity of solutions to human suffering which is brought about by respective religions can be a compromise between them so that a better solution is found to issues of the day.

This explanation shows that Gadamer's dialogue and the mutuality model both emphasise that to respond to diversity in the world, which is caused by human finitude is not based on unity, for unity is impossible, but is based on the compromises of many people who have full values concerning this life, and that this is possible. However, the mutuality model with its bridges seems to state that there is a common religious experience. This idea leads people to say that we will have the same understanding of the world if we view the three bridges. However, from Gadamer's perspective, this means that they want people to have understanding outside of their traditions, and this is really impossible in the light of human finitude.

The Acceptance Model

Previously, it was elaborated that the mutuality model emphasises something in common for the sake of obtaining a good life. The acceptance model, according to Knitter, stresses that the variety of religious traditions has to be accepted, but it refuses to follow the mutuality model—search

---

41. As quoted by Knitter, *Ibid.*
42. *Ibid,* 141.
43. *Ibid,* 140.

for a common ground—because for the acceptance model, this search for a common ground is both impossible as well as dangerous.

Postmodernism supports the ideas of the acceptance model. As stated before, Gadamer can be included in postmodernism on the one hand but criticises it on the other. According to postmodern thinkers, reasoning is able to bring human beings to agreement about truth but it is very easily contaminated and exploited. Furthermore, there is no one understanding that fits all cultures. Because 'facts always come in different cultural guises', one cannot ask for 'nothing but the facts'.[44] For postmodernism, the way to understand human beings and their life cannot be formulated as the mutuality model suggests because it is not only impossible but also dangerous to follow this line of thinking.

In refusing the mutuality model, the acceptance model argues that the many cannot be the one. Although diversity can be related and driven into 'unifying relationship', diversity is never separate from our selves. In other words, we are always together with diversity wherever we are.[45]

Gadamer agrees with the idea that reason is not free, it depends on previous reasoning sequence. This does not mean that reason does not have an important function. Reason is needed to determine true experiences. Besides that, the many, of course, cannot be one, and for Gadamer, to be one is not the aim of dialogue—not to adapt two standpoints but to compromise the possible truth.

The acceptance model warns that if we think that there is 'one absolute truth', we will never recognise it altogether.[46] This is because human experience and knowledge passes through various filters. This means that what we say as 'universal' truth is always understood through a certain filter.[47] The various filters lead to consequences in human life, as Knitter points out:

> The differences between our cultural-religious filters are so great that, for the most part, they are 'incommensurable'. That's a heavy-duty word for a heavy-duty claim. Its main message is that because each of us looks at the world (and the Divine) through our own cultural-religious glasses, and because, as historians and anthropologists tell us, these glasses

44. *Ibid,* 174.
45. *Ibid,* 177.
46. *Ibid,* 175.
47. *Ibid,* 176.

are so very, very different, and because it seems impossible for anyone to come up with a prescription for a pair of glasses that everyone would need and could wear, you can't judge one worldview in the light of other.[48]

In addition, to say that a universal truth exists means that we have to abolish other cultures, and is why the mutuality model becomes dangerous.[49]

In line with these ideas, Gadamer states that other truth claims can be regarded as a form of possible truth, but he still believes that universal truth exists and it leads us to continuously make an effort for the sake of attaining a better life. Gadamer also stresses that human finitude should not make us pessimistic in our pursuits, but it should make us optimistic by persistently trying to find the universal truth. This leads humans to be creative and to achieve a better understanding of their life. Nevertheless, he reminds us that we always understand life in the context of tradition.

The acceptance model is supported in the ideas of a number of other thinkers such as Lindbeck, Griffith, Heim and Clooney. According to Lindbeck, because language comes before experience, language plays the central role in human experience and knowledge.[50] This is the reason we cannot say that the divine is one, and this is what requires the fulfillment and mutuality models to be ultimately rejected. Based on this, language has an important position in our religious life. Our religious language enables us to experience and form our religious convictions.[51] It shows that since language is indeed different, it leads us to different worlds. The same words such as God or divine in all religions are understood differently, therefore one religious language cannot be translated to other religious languages, as all religious languages are 'untranslatable'.[52] Lindbeck emphasises that when one religion tries to say something in another religious language, the result is 'babbling'.[53] In Lindbeck's view 'no religion can be measured by another'.[54]

For Gadamer, experiences need to be expressed in language. He stresses that language makes us understand the world. In addition, people who

---

48. *Ibid*, 176–177
49. *Ibid*, 175.
50. Georg Lindbeck, *the Nature of Doctrine: Religion and Theology in a Postliberal Age* (Philadelphia: Wetminster, 1984), 40.
51. *Ibid*, 49.
52. As quoted by Knitter in *Introducing Theologies of Religions*, 181.
53. Lindbeck, *the Nature of Doctrine*, 42.
54. Knitter, *Introducing Theologies of Religions*, 182.

have different linguistic traditions will view the world in different ways. This implies that although humans may find similar religious experiences, they will have different expressions influenced by their backgrounds etc and so consequently humans will have different concepts of truth.

To say that there are no common grounds among religions, and that it is impossible to understand and criticise other religions, does not mean that this acceptance model aims to create walls between religions, but it strives to maintain and care for the real differences between world religions or faiths.[55] For this reason, religions have to be good neighbors:

> Religions are to be good neighbors to each other. But to do that, each of them needs to recognise that, indeed, 'good fences make good neighbors.' Each religion has its own backyard. There is no 'commons' that all of them share. To be good neighbors, then, let each religion tend to its own backyard, keeping in clean and neat.[56]

For this reason the followers of one religion can express what they think and this is the background for talking to the others. All have to listen to each other, and maybe this can be said to be a conversation. Nevertheless, there are no rules and agenda in the conversation as it just happens.[57] Based on this thought, dialogue is about the importance of feelings and thoughts, and they come together and just see what happens. Rules are not necessary, but 'ingenuity and trust' are.[58] This kind of 'conversation' leads people to understand their own uniqueness differently which then leads them to change things regarding their religious environment.

This understanding of dialogue aims at something similar to what Gadamer's claims. That is, that people 'fall into dialogue' and an effective dialogue can be undertaken without the control of any one person. Nevertheless, this idea does not lead Gadamer to go on and say that there are no rules in dialogue. Even, when the acceptance model says that there are no rules, it becomes the rule. As discussed in the preceding chapter, Gadamer provides several requirements such as using the same language and openness.

---

55. *Ibid*, 182.
56. *Ibid*, 183.
57. *Ibid*, 185.
58. *Ibid*.

Different to Lindbeck, who states that different languages among religions cause religions to truly differ, Heim asserts that since religions are really different, there are various languages.[59]

Heim believes that various goals lead to various eternal goals, it even indicates that there are different ultimates.[60] In other words, the diversity in God causes the diversity in religion.[61] This diversity brings us to have a relationship. 'There is no being without difference and communion.'[62]

In this sense, Gadamer has the same idea that differences drive human beings to engage in a relationship in terms of dialogue. This expands our horizon so that we understand the world around us better and are able to have a balance in how we measure our views against those of others.

The diversity of religions, according to Heim, means religious people are different, and we cannot say that we agree or do not agree. What can be done is to open ourselves and come to new understandings. Heim regards other superior truth claims of others as being valid in their own cultural-religious context in terms of being 'partially grasped'.[63]

Gadamer supports the idea that openness causes people to want to learn about and from others. This openness also enlarges our horizons and leads to new understandings. Without openness, people will claim that others are inferior but this claim is inevitable because not all humans are aware of their finitude, and this always happens when it is related to religious issues.

Every religion claims to possess the superior truth. As a result, the followers of a particular religion want to spread that conviction to those around them. If this were to happen, Heim suggests, it should not be a conflict nor religious arrogance, as each religion permits members of other religions to become missionaries and vice versa.[64] By allowing this dialogue leads to a new understanding of both oneself and other religions, and a social and ethical change for overcoming human suffering is created.

In line with this idea, from Gadamer's perspective people compromise to overcome problems of the world through dialogue. Therefore, the claims that one religion has the universal truth should not disrupt

---

59. See S Mark Heim, *Salvations: Truth and Difference in Religions,* 149–151.
60. *Ibid*, 153–157.
61. *Ibid*.
62. Heim, as quoted by Knitter *In Introducing Theologies of Religions,* 195.
63. *Ibid*, 198.
64. Heim, *Salvations: Truth and Difference in Religions,* 222.

dialogue. Although dialogue becomes a debate, it still brings us to compromise about what is good for human life. Dialogue also leads us to reconsider our opinions, which is why a dialogue indeed relates to our own opinions.

Besides Lindbeck and Heim, Griffith also reinforces the background of the acceptance model. He argues that deep in the believers' hearts, they defend their particular religion as the best religion. Thus, what is needed is that people state courteously, but precisely, their views when they say other believers are wrong. Through this kind of model, a significant and enjoyable conversation occurs. As a result, an interreligious dialogue at the same time is an interreligious apology occurs in terms of 'defense' or 'formal justification', one in which all participants defend their own belief as more 'comprehensive' than the other person or groups belief.[65] This easily leads to a misunderstanding that there is a change in a participants' mind, but Griffith emphasises that this is in fact very possible because this type of dialogue is based on a free flow of 'give and take' on both sides.

For Gadamer, dialogue is never a battle in defense of each participant's opinions. Dialogue occurs not to defend our own opinions, it serves no other purpose than to understand the others opinions. By only defending our own opinions, we cannot hope to understand the others opinions properly. In addition, Gadamer realises that we cannot measure the others' heart, which is why he stresses that a true dialogue depends on the participants' sincerity. Nevertheless, from Gadamer's point of view, to hold to the idea that our own religion has within it the only truth is allowed, but in dialogue, questions are not addressed to defend or prove that idea.

Another supporter of the acceptance model is Clooney. He regards interreligious dialogue as comparative theology. He states that in comparing one religion to another religious believers can learn from other religions. According to Clooney, the work of the comparative theologian is:

> extended and laborious, but also engaging and exciting, [a] process of passing over personally into the world of another religion, exploring that world, letting its symbols and stories seep into one's imagination, and then passing back to one's own religion to see what might happen.[66]

---

65. Knitter, *Introducing Theologies of Religions,* 186.
66. As quoted by Knitter, *Introducing Theologies of Religions,* 208.

Clooney asserts that comparative religious work, people return to their home with a new understanding and awareness which they also extend to their own lives. Clooney argues that in this model the followers of other religions become friends. We not only learn and share with them but also agree and learn to disagree with them.[67]

It seems that Clooney's thought is in line with Gadamer's concerning the idea of learning from each other, but to Gadamer, a new understanding is obtained when dialogue goes on, not only after it.

Understanding of different religions, for Clooney, is regarded as the 'cultural linguistic voice'.[68] When we hold a view that other religions are more valuable than ours, it is understandable through our own religion. This is because truth is never naked, it is always with a linguistic costume besides its own cultures and systems. The evaluation of truth claims may come but it takes a very long endeavor in understanding others' truth claims in our own language and context.

Clooney's concept of truth is very similar to Gadamer's. For Gadamer, tradition enables us to understand the world, therefore, truth occurs in tradition. This fact becomes the reason why what we view as a truth is always a possible truth. Nevertheless, the universal truth exists and throughout human life, humans strive to attain it. Gadamer's thought is close to the acceptance model of interreligious dialogue in the way that they understand the fact of human finitude. Nevertheless, Gadamer's response to human finitude is a bit different to the followers of the acceptance model of human finitude, Gadamer provides the requirements of the dialogue while they do not.

The exploration of Knitter's four models of interreligious dialogue in accordance to Gadamer's thought of human finitude shows that Gadamer's idea of human finitude is closer to the concept of the acceptance model although both are different in offering the model of dialogue. Meanwhile the people who follow the replacement model seem to disregard human finitude. People who prefer the fulfillment model try to understand human finitude in a positive way but they collapse the world into the superior and the inferior positions in the beginning of any dialogue. And, finally, people who work from the mutuality model try to go beyond human finitude by maintaining that if we use three bridges, philosophy, ethics and mysticism, we can find a common goal. This means whatever someone's tradition, culture and language are, they will find the common goal of re-

---

67. *Ibid*, 210–211.
68. *Ibid*, 212.

ligion. From Gadamer's perspective, this means to try understand another from outside of their tradition and this he argues is impossible because human understanding is always within tradition.

Concluding Remarks

The discussion on Gadamer's concept of human finitude and interreligious dialogue in the preceding chapters brings up a number of conclusions and leads to other discussions. I will divide this last chapter into three sections. The first section concerns human finitude and the need for dialogue, wherein the summary of the previous discussion of Gadamer's concept of human finitude is once again reiterated.

The second section relates to the discussion of the most adequate model of interreligious dialogue. In this section I will outline the requirements for dialogue according to Gadamer, and the association of these requirements to Knitter's four models of interreligious dialogue. Consequently, I also take a look at Knitter's ideas of interreligious dialogue. In addition, I provide my views related to interreligious dialogue based on my exploration of Gadamer's concept of human finitude and Knitter's four models of interreligious dialogue.

The third, and last, section describes how my exploration in earlier chapters is truly useful in the Indonesian context. I present the discussion of a conflict related to religious issues general, and the conflict in Maluku in particular as an example of the ideas outline in this book. The conflict is outline in terms of Knitter's four models of interreligious dialogue and Gadamer's concept of human finitude.

Human Finitude and the Need for Dialogue

According to Gadamer, humans are finite beings. The finitude is human reason and is shown through tradition, experience and language. These three facets of human finitude are respectively inseparable.

Gadamer argue that being part of a tradition is a part of being human. When humans are born, they will forever bear identities because they come into a world where tradition has been constructed in time and place. Thus, tradition is a human pre-condition. Aside from that, with tradition being part of being human, all people are involved in both its production and in its evolution.

Tradition comes from valid human experiences which cannot oppose new experience. In other words, the confrontation of old experience and new occurs thus achieving true experiences. True experiences are the experiences which broaden our horizons. Usually, we experience something which is out of our expectation. Nevertheless, this experience is full of value since it makes us knowledgeable. Therefore, the experienced person is a person who is radically undogmatic. This is because s/he truly learns from his/her experience. Although we can learn from our experiences, we are incapable of repeating it. However, what humans can do is to regenerate these 'true' experiences. This process is called reversal consciousness. Experience shows human finitude, and an experienced person is truly aware of this.

An experience becomes impossible to be understood if it is not expressed in language. In other words, humans can understand their experiences only through language. Therefore, only language can describe reality. Through the means of language, humans have the ability to understand the world. In addition, understanding between human beings happens through language. Nevertheless, due to the limitations of human reason, although humans apply various words to describe their thoughts, they still face the problem of a lack of words. This variety of words leads humans to have different concepts in viewing the world. Thus, people who have different linguistic traditions view the world in different manners because language itself shows reality and the other language is the basis of human understanding.

Human finitude has several consequences. The first is that the process of human understanding is always within a particular tradition. Humans cannot understand something outside of a particular reference of a tradition since human understanding substantially depends on previous presuppositions which are inherited through tradition. Tradition makes it possible for humans to overcome their problems. This idea does not lead to the undermining of the function of human reason because 'true' tradition needs reasonable consideration. Thus, reason determines the most adequate tradition leading to a good life. Nevertheless, people have to realise that reason does not stand freely, it depends on previous reasoning sequences.

The second consequence of human finitude concerns truths. The fact that human understanding is always within the scope of tradition means that human understanding starts from history. Therefore, humans are basically historical beings. In the process of understanding, there is a fusion of past and present. The past horizon originates those who have gone before us and have provided some definitions to the things that we see and experience throughout our lifetimes. Thus, understanding is always changing and developing and as a result truth becomes more of a historical process. All opinions are relative in nature, and what are regarded as truths are always only possible truths. Nevertheless, this reality should not lead people to be pessimistic, on the contrary, it should lead people to be otherwise, to be optimistic. People should never stop trying to find truths in their lifetime since universal truth remains.

The third consequence is that prejudice arises in the encounter of people who have different traditions, experiences and languages. It is only natural that when the process of understanding occurs, prejudices will arise. Prejudice is not to be avoided because it is a bias of human openness to the world. This does not mean that humans have to accept prejudices without consideration. Prejudice is merely a starting point to understand something, thus it still needs to be differentiated between legitimate prejudice and illegitimate prejudice. Legitimate prejudice is prejudice which we regard as a principle of life and we believe it can bring us to a good life. Legitimate prejudice is attained from dialogue. Therefore, as participants in a dialogue, we have to postpone our own prejudices before the process of dialogue can occur. If we do not examine our prejudices through dialogue, our prejudices still become illegitimate because prejudices are often in error.

The description above seems to show that there is no problem with human finitude and its consequences. Nevertheless, in the encounter of various traditions, experiences and languages, there is undeniably potential for conflict to occur. Prejudices are not only the beginning of engaging in a dialogue, but it is prone to start a conflict as well.

The Most Adequate Model of Interreligious Dialogue

The reality above is the real reason to engage in dialogue. We can understand each other because dialogue enables us to clarify these prejudices and it makes us aware of what we need in order to create a good life. In order for dialogue to function properly, Gadamer provides several requirements. The first is that participants use the same language. Certainly, to understand each other, the participants use the same language, hence misunderstanding can hopefully be avoided. Using the same language enables the participants to enter the language game through the dialectic of questioning and answering.

The second requirement is that no participant of dialogue controls the conversation. If one of the participants controls the conversation, a true conversation will not occur because the outcome of the conversation would only suffice to the controller's willingness. Hence, the conversation becomes useless.

The third requirement is that someone does not impel his/her standpoints onto the other. A participant should not impel his/her standpoint onto the other participant because the aim of conversation is not to find the same standpoint. If each participant has different standpoints, there can always be compromise. Thus, the participants focus is on inquiring a powerful argument, instead of defending his/her argument or defeating the other's.

The fourth requirement is for the participants to focus on the core of discussion. Only by focusing on the core of dialogue, can a true dialogue be attained. Each participant must concentrate on the discussion so that his/her statements are aimed at possible truths.

The fifth requirement concerns openness. Each participant has to be open to his/her own self in terms of listening, learning and responding. This means that each participant should want to learn and understand the other's statement which in turn brings him/her to respond to the statement. The openness is indicated by each participant acknowledging that there is value in the other persons opinions. Thus, they listen to each other, not just hear what is said.

The sixth requirement is related to questions and answers during the conversation. The questions and the answers are aimed at finding truths and clarifying prejudices. In addition, the questions require a new knowledge and maintain the orientation of openness.

The last requirement is that participants have to be aware of these requirements. The awareness of these requirements means conversations can function properly.

Concerning interreligious dialogue, Gadamer's ideas on human finitude makes us aware of others, and this is without a doubt necessary before we engage in dialogue with others. Moreover, his thought helps us in considering the models of interreligious dialogue and gives pointers to the most proper and effective model of dialogue to create a good life.

If we link Gadamer's requirements of dialogue based on his thought of human finitude to Knitter's four models of interreligious dialogue, it is not easy to say that one of them is the most adequate model because each model shows different points of view in interreligious dialogue. Nevertheless, Gadamer's concept of human finitude is more closely associated with the acceptance model than any of the other models. In addition, dialogue which is offered by the followers of this model is the very similar if not the same as Gadamer's idea of 'falling into conversation'. Nevertheless, Gadamer provides several requirements of dialogue which are not found in these models.

From Gadamer's perspective, there is something 'disturbing' in the replacement model because each participant impels his/her own standpoint onto the other. S/he wants the other to follow his/her standpoint. In other words, there is no compromise in this model. In addition, participants in this model focus on persuading the other to have the same standpoint that they do. Thus, participants do not acknowledge the other's opinion as a value, making it difficult to garner a good response in this model because questions and answers are aimed at convincing the other party to change their perspective/opinion. Nevertheless, these ideas really show the honesty and conviction.

From Gadamer's point of view, the distorted question still poses as an obstructive thing in the fulfillment model. However, the followers of the fulfillment model make us understand human finitude; they truly regard that others have values.

People, who follow the mutuality model, think that there is common ground looking out of one's own tradition, and this is impossible for Gadamer. Even so, they push us to take positive and constructive actions: we do not only come together to engage in a dialogue and to cooperate in promoting human well-being but also to appreciate diversity.

From his discussion of the four models of interreligious dialogue, Knitter conveys two steps of interreligious dialogue. The first step is to relate religions to ethics. This means that the followers of different religions come together to overcome the problems of human suffering. They do not talk about their beliefs but the application of their religious messages in abolishing suffering and violence.[1]

The second step, according to Knitter, is to share religious belief. This step is related to the first; by coming together it will lead the followers of different religions to share their religious beliefs. The goal of sharing is not to find which beliefs are true, but for the sake of helping victims of violence. Thus, all people accept differences and tensions but they always learn from others.[2]

I realise that although Knitter's four models of interreligious dialogue seem to represent the phenomena in society, we will find more complicated phenomena in reality. Nevertheless, these models lead people to learn how to engage in interreligious dialogue and make them reconsider their attitude towards others.

Returning to the discussion of Gadamer's concept of human finitude and interreligious dialogue, how does this function in the world? In Indonesia, for instance, there are many different religions and belief systems. That there are encounters between the followers of different religions is inevitable. The differences have potential for conflict because there exists people with strong views and there are also some irresponsible people who use religious issues to create social, religious based, conflict. One of the possible measures to avoid the conflict is through dialogue. In my view, people in Indonesia can choose their own model for dialogue, from Knitter's models or the any other model. However, I suggest that the awareness of otherness is crucial in engaging in any interreligious dialogue. In other words, it should function well if people are aware of human finitude.

I acknowledge that there is no guarantee that if all people were aware of human finitude and its implications, violence and conflict would not occur because causes of violence and conflict originate from complex situations. Nevertheless, the awareness of otherness would help us to understand each other and to create good relations with others.

In conclusion, people, in my mind, are free to choose one of the models of Knitter's four models of interreligious dialogue. We cannot impel someone to choose the most adequate model according to our experi-

---

1. Paul F Knitter, *Introducing Theologies of Religions*, (Maryknoll, NY: Orbis Books, 2002), 244.
2. *Ibid.*

ence and exploration. In addition, I think that an interreligious dialogue between two people who chose different models of interreligious dialogue can occur. Therefore, what we have to realise is that we are indeed not without limitations.

A Brief Discussion on Human Finitude and Interreligious Dialogue in the Indonesian Context

Before closing our discussion on human finitude and interreligious dialogue, I would like to provide a brief discussion on the topic in relation to the Indonesian context. As mentioned in the beginning of this chapter, I pose the conflict in Maluku as an example because it was a considerable case and it consumed a large amount of time in finding the solution.

Throughout Indonesian history, many cultural, ethnic and religious conflicts occur. According to Garang, the sentiment in terms of culture, ethnicity and religion increases, widens, and spreads in Indonesia, and he found that religious sentiment is dominant.[3] In addition, religious factors can be a source of violence and conflict. It has been proven that fanatics of religious teaching rapidly increase the state of conflicts and violence.[4] Many people believe that behind religious conflict, there is a political interest. As widely assumed, in Indonesia it is difficult to separate religion and politics because religion is one of the supporting factors of political interest.[5]

In recent years there have been several conflicts involving the followers of different religions, and the case of violence in Maluku has been a significant conflict in Indonesia. The conflict started in the beginning of 1999 and showed progress towards finding a solution in the beginning of 2002. During the conflict, thousands of people died, many houses and buildings were destroyed.

Many scholars conducted research on the cause of the Maluku conflict. Although there are significant differences in regards to the cause, many theories state that the conflict started from a conflict between two people from different religious traditions. Pieris considers it is extremely easy for a conflict among followers of different religions, namely Muslims and Christians, to turn into something serious due to the extreme sensi-

---

3. J Garang in John Pieris, *Tragedi Maluku: Sebuah Krisis Peradaban*. (Jakarta: Yayasan Obor Indonesia, 2004), 17.
4. *Ibid*, 19.
5. Hotmann Siahaan, in Pieris *Tragedi Maluku: Sebuah Krisis Peradaban*, 19.

tivity of religious issues on both sides.[6] If there is a follower of one religion who gets hurt, his/her comrades will usually take action without clarifying the cause. In addition, according to Pieris the government did not take sufficient steps in solving this conflict, and they did not seem serious in overcoming the violence and the conflict.[7] However, Pieris believes that conflict in Maluku is ultimately due to political interests.[8] Religious issues are only a tool to raise tensions among the conflicting parties because it is somewhat effective to further complicate the conflict. Nevertheless, I am not concerned in discussing this conflict deeply because it is not the focus of the book, but in this last section I want to propose the possibility of the application of interreligious dialogue and human finitude to the conflict.

Pieris argues that there were four realities which became a background of the conflict in Maluku, that is social, religious, cultural, and political realities.[9] Because this book is concerned with religious issues, I will only examine the religious reality in Maluku. Pieris's suggests that there are three religious characteristics of Maluku people. The first is that both Muslims and Christians are exceptionally pious people, and that their religious values become their life principles. The second is that they believe and regard the followers of other religions as infidels and believe that those of another religion are not following God's will. The last characteristic is that they are entrapped in religious symbolism while they do not completely understand the symbolism. There is potential for conflict when these religious symbolisms are 'disturbed'.[10]

The characteristics above became a factor to make the conflict significant. Moreover, according to Pieris religious figures were not ready to lead their followers in resolving the issues, and were even involved in the conflict.[11]

As stated previously, one of the possible measures to avoid conflict is through dialogue and so here I would like to cross reference to Knitter's four models of interreligious dialogue with the conflict in Maluku.

Based on the characteristics of the religious outline in Maluku, the ideas of the followers of the replacement model would seem to be domi-

---

6. John Pieris, *Tragedi Maluku: Sebuah Krisis Peradaban* (Jakarta: Yayasan Obor Indonesia, 2004), 36–37.
7. *Ibid*, 60–61.
8. *Ibid*, 98.
9. *Ibid*, 73–109.
10. *Ibid*, 82.
11. *Ibid*, 145.

nant. This model, as has been noted, holds, among other things, the belief that it is God's will that there is only one religion while the followers of other religions are lost. In other words, some both of the Muslims and Christians in this community held the belief that their own religion is the only true religion. Thus, during the dialogue that occurred in and after the conflict, Muslims and Christians competed to show that their faith was the only one true. In this particular competition, each participant was being honest, open and respectful. It is possible to have understanding among Muslims and Christians but it has potential to create a clear and wide separation between Muslims and Christians because as Gadamer reminds us, there is something 'bothering' in this model: each participant aims to replace the other. This means that Muslims and Christians defended their opinion as the only true religion and wanted the other to follow them and abandon the religious faith they had until then..

If people in Maluku had followed the fulfillment model, this would mean that in the dialogue Muslims would invite Christians to follow their religious truth, and Christians would persuade Muslims to follow them. Although they would acknowledge that the other has values in their own religion and the dialogue would be conducted in a respectful manner towards each other. But perhaps, it would not a good idea to implement this in Maluku because people in Maluku are so pious that this is very disturbing prospect. As Gadamer reminds us, the aim of dialogue is not to defend and reinforce our own opinions. Can understanding between Muslims and Christian occur if each of them focuses on the need to invite the other to have the same opinion and thus change religion?

The mutuality model would seem to be a proper model to have been followed by people in Maluku because in this model, Muslims and Christian come together to overcome human problems by examining common ground. To find the solution of human problems, Muslims and Christians show how their own religion provides a proper solution to the problem. Can this be accepted by all people so that the other religion can be understood as having a better solution to human problems? However, this model truly maintains diversity. Perhaps, this is what Moluccans needed, although from Gadamer's perspective, it is hard to say that there is a common ground among religions because people indeed have different experiences which lead them to different concepts of truth.

If Moluccans preferred the acceptance model, Muslims and Christians alike would have come to realise human finitude, which consequently would have let other people have their own religious belief, and not be disturbed by them or those of the others. This would have been a dialogue were both Muslims and Christians allowed dialogue to occur naturally without determining the requirements of that dialogue. This model might be fit the Maluku case but it seems that it does not provide post conflict solution. From Gadamer's point of view, the requirements of dialogue are still needed to make dialogue work well so that understanding, compromises and clarification are actually possible.

A short description of the case above raises several questions. Due to the religious characteristics of Moluccans which are close to the ideas of the replacement model, would Moluccans have chosen the replacement model? How would dialogue occur if various models of interreligious dialogue had been chosen? If people thought that one of the models was the right and proper one to be applied in Maluku, is it possible to ask everyone to choose that model? However, the short description of the conflict and the models possibilities in this conflict are both artificial and simplistic. Therefore, we need further research and a comprehensive discussion to find the proper type of dialogue to be applied in Indonesia both before and after a conflict occurs such as the one in Malaku.

In my view, the awareness of the otherness related to human finitude is useful in whatever models of interreligious dialogue Moluccans could take. In other words, it is better for participants to have the awareness of otherness or the awareness of human finitude before they come to any dialogue. If Maluccans were aware of human finitude, they would think that they are really finite. They would realise that although they live in the same place, they have different experiences and different traditions. This would cause them to be different in viewing the world around them. In other words, they would also be aware of others' views of the world through the other telescope, the telescope of the other. If they have this awareness, in dialogue they should not impart their own opinion on to others. They would be open to each other because their aim is to understand each other and to find the solution to their problems.

But this is not without problems; for instance, how would you make Maluccans realise human finitude and have an awareness of otherness? What process of formation, what type of program would be developed and by whom and with whom to come to this result? Who would lead this type of process and where and how would it occur? Moreover, although the people might realise human finitude, which one of concepts would they take because it is possible they might have different concepts about human finitude? Finally, how far can the awareness of otherness help to minimise conflict and violence because there are other factors which lead to violence in so many instances?

Maluku is only one of the examples, there are many places in Indonesia and the world which have potential for conflict or already have had conflict in the recent and not so recent past. However, we need other and further research to answer such questions above.

Bibliography

Ambrosio, Francis J. 'Gadamer, Plato, and the Discipline of Dialogue', in *International Philosophical Quarterly,* Vol XXVII, 1/105 (March 1987): 17–32.

_____. 'Gadamer and Aristotle: Hermeneutics as Participant in Tradition', in *Hermeneutic and the Tradition,* edited by Daniel O Dahlstrom (Washington: The American Catholic Philosophical Association, 1988).

Bertens, Kees. *Filsafat Abad XX: Inggris-Jerman* (Jakarta: Gramedia, 1990).

Bontekoe, Ron. 'A Fusion of Horizons: Gadamer and Schleiermacher', in *International Philosophical Quarterly,* Vol XXVII, 1/105 (March 1987): 3–16.

Bullock, Jeffrey F. 'Preaching in a Postmodern Wor[l]d: Gadamer's Philosophical Hermeneutics as Homiletical Conversation', in *Christian Theological Seminary Research Group.* http://home.apu.edu/~CTRF/paper/1997_paper/bullock.html.

Cameron, WSK. 'On Communicative Actors Talking Past One Another: The Gadamer-Habermas Debate', in *Philosophy Today,* Spring (1996): 160–167.

Carr, Thomas K. *Newman and Gadamer: Toward a Hermeneutics of Religious Knowledge* (Atlanta, Georgia: Scholars Press, 1996).

Cassier, E. *The Philosophy of The Enlightenment,* translated and edited by FCA Coellen and JP Pettegrove (Boston: Beacon Press, 1995).

Cohen, Andrew. 'Knowledge, Power, and Enlightenment', http://www.wie.org/j11/kpe.asp.

Fairfield, Paul. 'Truth Without Methodologism: Gadamer and James', in *American Catholic Philosophical Quarterley,* Vol LXVII 3 (1993): 285–297.

Gadamer, Hans-Georg. *Truth and Method*, translated by Garret Barden and John Cumming (New York: Seabury Press, 1975).

_____. 'The Problem of Historical Consciousness', in *Interpretive Social Science: A Reader*, edited by Paul Robinow and William M Sullivan (Berkeley and London: University of California Press, 1979).

_____. *Philosophical Hermeneutics*, translated and edited by David E Linge (London: University of California Press, 1977).

_____. 'The Historicity of Understanding', in *The Hermeneutics Reader: Texts of the German Tradition from Enlightenment to the Present*, translated and edited by Kurt Mueller Volmer (New York: Continuum, 1985).

_____. *On the Circle of Understanding*, in *Hermeneutics Versus Science? Three German Views*, edited and translated by John M Connolly and Thomas Keutner (Notre Dame, IND: University of Notre Dame Press, 1988).

_____. *Gadamer in Conversation: Reflection and Commentary*, edited and translated by Richard E Palmer (New Haven and London: Yale University Press, 2001).

Gay, Peter. A*bad Pencerahan* (Jakarta: Tira Pustaka, 1984).

Grondin, Jean. *Hans-Georg Gadamer: Biography* (New Haven and London: Yale University Press, 2003).

_____. *The Philosophy of Gadamer* (Montreal & Kingston: McGill-Queen's University Press, 2003).

Giurlanda, Paul FSC. 'Habermas' Critique of Gadamer: Does it Stand Up?', in *International Philosophical Quarterly*, Vol XXVII, 1/105 (March 1987): 33–41.

Hans, James S. 'Hans-Georg Gadamer and Hermeneutic Phenomenology', in *Philosophy Today*, 22 (1978): 3–19.

Hardiman, F Budi. *Melampaui Positivisme dan Modernitas* (Yogyakarta: Kanisius, 2003)

_____. *Filsafat Modern: Dari Machiavelli sampai Nietzsche* (Jakarta: Gramedia Pustaka Utama, 2004).

_____. *Kritik Ideologi: Pertautan Pengetahuan dan Kepentingan* (Yogyakarta: Kanisius, 1990).

Healy, Paul. 'Situated Rationality and Hermeneutics Understanding: A Gadamerian Approach to Rationality', in *International Philosophical Quarterly*, Vol XXXVI, 2 /142 (June 1996): 155–171.

Heim, S Mark. *Salvations: Truth and Difference in Religion* (Maryknoll, NY: Orbis Books, 1995).

Henry, Martin. 'The Enlightenment and Romanticism from a Theological Perspective', in *Irish Theological Quartely*, 63/3 (1998): 250–262.

Hick, John. *An Interpretation of Religion: Human Responses to the Transcendent* (Basingstoke: Macmillan, 1989).

_____. *Problems of Religious Pluralism* (London: Macmillan, 1985).

Hogan, John P. 'Gadamer and the Hermeneutical Experience', in *Philosophy Today*, 20 (1976): 3–12.

_____'Hermeneutics and The Logic of Question and Answer: Collingwood and Gadamer', in *Heythrop Journal*, XXVIII (1987): 263–284.

Jervolino, Domenico. 'Gadamer and Ricoeur on the Hermeneutics of Praxis', in *The Hermeneutics of Action*, edited by Richard Kearney (London: SAGE Publication, 1996).

Johnson, Patricia Alternbernd. 'Gadamer: Incarnation, Finitude and the Experience of Divine Infinitude', in *Faith and Philosophy*, 10/4 (October 1993): 539–552.

Kisiel, Theodore. 'The Happening of Tradition: The Hermeneutics of Gadamer and Heidegger', in *Man and World 2* (1969): 358–385.

_____. 'The Happening of Tradition: The Hermeneutics of Gadamer and Heidegger', in *Hermeneutics and Praxis,* edited by Robert Hollinger (Notre Dame, IND: University of Notre Dame Press,1985).

Knitter, F Paul. *Introducing: Theologies of Religions* (Maryknoll, NY: Orbis Books, 2002).

Kurtz, Lester R. *God in the Global Village: The World's Religions in Sociological Perspective* (California: Pine Forge Press, 1995).

Lawrence, Frederick. 'Gadamer and Lonergan: A Dialectical Comparison', in *International Philosophical Quarterly,* 20 (1980): 25–47.

Lindbeck, Georg. *The Nature of Doctrine: Religion and Theology in a Postliberal Age* (Philadelphia: Westminster Press, 1984).

Linge, David. 'Hans-Georg Gadamer', *Philosophical Hermeneutics* (London: University of California Press, 1977).

Madison, Gary Brent. 'Hermeneutics and (the) Tradition', in *Hermeneutic and the Tradition,* edited by Daniel O Dahlstrom (Washington: The American Catholic Philosophical Association, 1988).

Misgeld, Dieter. 'On Gadamer's Hermeneutics', in *Hermeneutics and Praxis,* edited by Robert Hollinger (Notre Dame, IND: University of Notre Dame Press, 1985).

Murchadha, Felix O. 'Truth as a Problem for Hermeneutics: Towards a Hermeneutical Theory of Truth', in *Philosophy Today* (Summer 1992): 122–130.

Palmer, Richard E. *Gadamer in Conversation: Reflections and Commentary* (New Heaven & London: Yale University Press, 2001).

Pannenberg, Wolfhart. 'The Religious from the Perspective of Christian Theology and the Self-Interpretation of Christianity in Relation to Non-Christian Religions', in *Modern Theology,* 9 (1993): 285–297.

_____. *Basic Questions in Theology* (Philadelphia: Fortress Press, 1971).

Pieris, John. *Tragedi Maluku: Sebuah Krisis Peradaban* (Jakarta: Yayasan Obor Indonesia, 2004).

Rahner, Karl. 'Jesus Christ in Non-Christian Religions', in *Theological Foundations: An Introduction to the Idea of Christianity* (New York: Crossroad, 1978).

Schmidt, Lawrence. 'Hans-Georg Gadamer: A Biographical Sketch', in *Gadamer's Century: Essays in Honors of Hans-Georg Gadamer,* edited by Jeff Malpas, Ulrich Arnswald, and Jens Kertscher (London: MIT Press, 2002).

Schuchman, Paul. 'Aristotle's Phronesis and Gadamer's Hermeneutics', in *Philosophy Today*, 23 (1979): 41–50.

Swidler, Leonard. *After the Absolute: The Dialogical Future of Religious Reflection* (Minneapolis: Augsburg-Fortress Press, 1990).

Warnke, Georgia. *Gadamer: Hermeneutics, Tradition, and Reason* (Cambridge: Polity Press, 1987).

Weinsheimer, Joel C. *Gadamer's Hermeneutic: A Reading Truth and Method* (London: University of California Press, 1985).